# Clowning Glory

*Roly Bain and Patrick Forbes*

*Cartoons by Chic Jacob*

**National Society/Church House Publishing**

National Society/Church House Publishing
Church House
Great Smith Street
London
SW1P 3NZ

ISBN 0 7151 4863 X

First published in 1995 by The National Society and Church House Publishing



A British Library CIP record is available for this book.

Cover design by 2Q
Text design and typesetting by Church House Publishing
Printed in Great Britain by Biddles Ltd., Guildford and King's Lynn

# Contents


*Foreword* 5

Absurdity 7
Acrobats 7
Advent themes 8
All ages 9
Any old iron? 10
Auguste 11
Balance 12
Banners 14
Behave yourself! 14
The Bible . . . a barrel of laughs? 15
Bubbles 17
Build a mad machine 17
Children – don't scare them! 18
Christingle themes 20
Christmas themes 22
Clown 23
Clown bands 23
Clown biscuits 24
Clown car 24
Collages 25
Conviction counts 26
Costume ideas 27
Crosses and kisses 29
Diabolo 30
Drama as worship and vice versa 32
Easter cards 32
Eggs 33
Emotions 34
Evangelism and the clown . . . good news or bad? 36
Exaggeration 37
Facepaints 38
Falls 41
Feast of Fools – upside-down-ness 43
Feather dusters 44
Feet 45
Foolishness 46
Fun and games 46
Gravity and gravitas 48
Great clowns 48
Harvest ideas 50
Hats 51
Holy Fools UK history 53
Holy Week ideas 55
Improvisation 58
Indestructibility or resurrection 59
Innocence? 59
Innocent as doves? 60
Invention and imagination 60
Inversion of status 61
The jester 62
Jokes 63
Juggling 64
Kingship 67
K.I.S.S. 69
Knees 70
Knock-knock 70
Laughter 71
Letting go 72
Licence 73
Limericks 74
Lonely 75
Love 76
Madness 77
Magic 78
Masks 79
Michaelmas madness 80
Ministry 81
Mirrors 82
Names 83
Never mind jollity . . . be joyful 85
New eyes for old 86
Next to Godliness? 87
Noses 87

Objects, use of 88
Offence 89
Opera 89
Pies 91
Piety: good and bad 93
Plates 94
Play and playfulness 96
Prayer 97
Preparation 98
Prisons 99
Problem-solving 100
Processions and pomposity 101
Quality control 103
Questions 103
Resurrection 105
Risky business 106
Rola-bola 106
Rules 108
Saints 109
Silence! 110
Slapstick 110
Smile! 112
Stilts 113
Storytelling – a lost art? 114
Surprise 115
Symbol not structure 115
Tears 116
Timing is everything 117
Touch 118
Tragedy and comedy 119
Tramp clown 120
Trombone 121
Truthfulness 122
Under-rehearsed, underpaid . . . 123
Unicycle 124
Ventriloquism 125
Vestments 127
Vulnerability 128
Walks 129
Water 131
Welcome 132
Whiteface 133
Wig 134
Worship 135
Yes 136
Zoo games 137

*Bibliography* 139
*Useful addresses* 142

# Foreword

Roly and Patrick are a strong whiff of the 'clowning glory'. If you believe that the Christian faith is like a strait-jacket, worship like the atmosphere in a railway station waiting room, and church services like an undertaker's wake, then this book is not for you. On the other hand, perhaps it could reach parts that other books don't reach. I know, to my own cost and delight, that these two clowns have a sort of Godspell way of helping us to see the funny side of ourselves, of pricking pomposity, of discovering the laughter in heaven. I know because I've been custard pied by Roly, and was convinced that Patrick's imitation of a seagull in response to inhuman planning when he was team vicar in Thamesmead was a truly sane reaction.

When I was first ordained, laughing in Church was regarded as almost sinful – a wry smile was allowed – just. Now the people of God are being freed up to smile and laugh and taste the wonderful humour of the God who made us; the God who also created foals to skip and chew coat buttons and tease, and Charlie Chaplin and Laurel and Hardy. Fun and clowning are not a God-free zone: it's all mixed up with the mystery and struggle of life. The best laughter often bubbles up at the hardest times.

This is a workbook to help people dare to free up, to encourage already-growing freedom and release the chains of unvaried formality. It is not about worship as entertainment, but it is dead against God being made boring or the exclusion of spontaneous fun in the loving relationship we have with God (imagine a fun-free relationship – a bit like the one I have with the Inland Revenue – ugh!). Neither does it seek to reduce the value of reverence or stillness or silence, rather it helps human beings to be brave enough to be themselves before him, and so to find these things all the more beautiful and full of God.

If there's no fun in heaven, do we want to go? Rather like church . . .

*The Right Reverend Jim Thompson*
*Bishop of Bath and Wells*

## Absurdity

What a wonderful beginning to an alphabet about clowns, because clowns are wonderfully absurd. They speak to us of things beyond the mundane and sensible and grey areas of life as we know it and take us into uncharted lands we hardly dare dream of. Absurd? Of course, it isn't. Clowns may not be the arbiters of good taste but they are the judges of authenticity, and many of the things that society sees as perfectly sensible and fair and just are revealed to be patently absurd by this foolish fellow. Clowns in their foolish antics present us with a mirror in which we see ourselves in all our absurdity. Clowns have to be absurd if only to show us how infinitely more absurd we are – at least the clown is absurd on purpose!

## Acrobats

Not everyone's a natural acrobat! Nevertheless, forward rolls, cartwheels, jumping through hoops etc., are always spectacular. Use them as ways of getting on stage, or just to brighten up the procession! Make sure you warm up first, and try to keep in trim so that you're fairly flexible. Acrobalances, where two people balance on each other in different positions, and human pyramids look good. If they are well-rehearsed they can culminate in choreographed clown collapses. Acrobatics help us to be physical and joyous – they're worth the effort! Wouldn't it be wonderful to see the clown as the lame or paralytic man healed by Jesus who then takes off down the aisle in acrobatic joy . . .

## Advent themes

Advent is a good time for clowns. Clowns get everything ready for Christmas, creating the atmosphere in which celebration can happen, caring for detail and pointing to more profound meanings and truths.

Clowns could prepare the church each week, dusting around, but also acting as sidespersons and dusting the people as they come in, making sure they're ready too. Add a new feature each week – a picture or symbol or banner. Use Advent candles, and make the last central candle an everlighting candle – the light that the darkness can never overcome, however hard we try to extinguish it. Clowns make sure that everything is just right. Equally, just as the birth of Christ turned the world upside down, maybe clowns could rearrange things a little each week – the furniture and the order of service – forcing us to look at things as well as faith from a different perspective.

Being awake and alert is a classic Advent theme, and clowns can always make sure that their congregations are awake and hopefully on the edge of their seats – clown bands come immediately to mind, but there are lots of other ways that clowns might test response. What about a huge clown mallet administered to the minister's knee to check his reactions?

The idea of waiting is another theme, and clowns with enormous pocket watches might have something to say – an impatient whiteface (*see* **Whiteface**) could be taught a lot by a contented auguste (*see* **Auguste**).

Tears might be another theme – the clown's trademark but also God's. Perhaps incorporating the theme of darkness into light, tears could turn from sorrow to joy, from frustration to fulfilment, from penitence to forgiveness. Make a banner that spells 'Advent' in teardrops, smiles and frowns.

John the Baptist features in the Advent readings – a classic tramp (*see* **Tramp clown**) character, dirty, ragged and smelly, living in the wilderness, shunned by society, and yet his is the prophetic voice. Scenarios involving John the Baptist as tramp, Jesus as auguste, and any number of pharisaic whitefaces would be rich in potential.

Finally, clowns and fools have often been seen as the messengers of and for God, so clowns as angels is a gift. Not only are there comic possibilities with wings and costumes, but there is the whole idea that it is such an absurd message that they bring – that God is being born in a stable in Bethelehem must be a joke, especially born to a virgin. And yet it is a divine joke that speaks volumes of the foolishness of God that is wiser than our wisdom. Just as the clowns are the jesters who nevertheless tell the truth, so are the angels too, and it is they who prepare us for the outrageously generous gift from God of himself.

## All ages

You're never too young or too old to be God's fool or Christ's clown. Just as God welcomes all ages, from the youngest child toddling towards the altar or an old woman on her deathbed struggling towards the truth, so everyone is welcome to God's world of clowns and fools. There's no fool like an old fool, and no clown like a young clown in God's kingdom, described by one American writer as a party.

I remember a lovely man, Ken Akers who, in his late fifties, joined a liturgical dance group and found all kinds of new insights about movement and prayer as he learned a new way of being. It changed his life as clowning and fooling have changed mine. I don't need to apologise for fooling and playing and clowning. I'm not tyrannised by what others think I should be doing as an adult as I look forward to retirement. Growing old gracefully and disgracefully looks like fun.

Children bring wonder and excitement and curiosity, and in some of us that child has been repressed even murdered by convention. Unless we become as little children, we shall never inherit the kingdom. Older people have so much to offer and yet we cripple them by our low expectations of them. Clowning and fooling can bring a new awareness of the gifts that God showers on us, young and old alike, and a new opportunity to celebrate and enjoy the gifts in one another.

Best of all, once we experience the joy of finding that we can be clowns and fools however young or old we are, we can offer that gift of inclusiveness to all we meet. If we are being offered a place by God, if we're acceptable, then so is everyone, young and old, high and low, the in-crowd, the outsiders and all those in between. Great!

## Any old iron?

One of the best sources for clown props is the humble jumble sale. Here you can find strange long things with a lump on the end. Nobody knows what it may be, but for a few pence it can become something strange and magical in a clown routine. Hats and bizarre articles of clothing, bought for almost nothing and then washed and ironed can transform a clown's outfit, as well as providing some income for a good cause. Alarm clocks that don't keep perfect time, radios that can be working one minute and then smashed to pieces with a large mallet the next . . . all have their place and their possibility.

Develop an eye for what might work with an audience: some dreadful gadget or innovation that barely lasted the trip home from the shop may make a powerful point about materialism. I've seen plastic recorders go for peanuts when they have years of music still left in them, and amazing hats looking suicidal over the little wear they've had. Charity shops are well worth searching though they are less likely to have the really outrageous rubbish you can find at the humble jumbles.

> **Danger Box**
>
> Keep a tight hold on any possessions you're carrying at a jumble! They are easily sold on if you foolishly put them down on a stall or table. I once pursued a handbag to the outskirts of Yeovil before retrieving it from someone to whom I'd mistakenly sold it!

## Auguste

When you think of a clown in your mind's eye you probably picture a clumsy circus clown with big boots, ill-fitting suit and a big red nose. Well, he's called an Auguste. He's the clown everything happens to – he's the one who's on the end of everything, especially custard pies, as well as being the chief mischief-maker. He's the funny man, apparently at the beck and call of the ringmaster or the whiteface clown, though of course he isn't really. He's guaranteed to make a mess of it, but he gains our sympathy because we somehow identify with him. He's the slapstick man. In circuses he's the glue that holds the show together, and without the

clowns the circus would be a very different place indeed. He's the one who doesn't take himself seriously.

Auguste is playful and good fun. The ever faithful and loyal servant of all, he keeps falling over, being tripped and tricked, getting things hugely wrong, but he gets there in the end. His is the triumph of hope over experience, and we're with him all the way. If you're going to be a clown, auguste is the most fun to be, but it comes with a few bruises too.

To be an auguste is to play with exaggeration. The clothes are too small or too big, the make-up on the face exaggerates what is already there, and the boots are the size they are because he keeps putting his big foot in it. Gestures are big, as are reactions and ideas. He doesn't do things by halves! He doesn't only just get it wrong, it's always an absolute disaster; and equally, when he gets it right it's a moment of sheer triumph. If you want to try to be an auguste, be big, have fun, and enjoy it – especially all the mistakes and disasters.

*(See also* **Facepaints** *for ideas for auguste faces,* **Costumes** *for obvious reasons,* **Falls** *so you don't hurt yourself,* **Nose** *if you want one,* **Pies** *if you want to throw one, and* **Slapstick** *if you're going to be really clever.)*

## Balance

If you've ever gasped in wonder as the woman at the circus balanced a tray of glasses, filled with water if not the finest champagne, on the end of a tall pole or a sword or some such, on her chin, then you should try it! In a very short time you'll be able to make your friends gasp too.

Take a broomstick and stand it on the palm of your hand, or on the end of your finger. Now as long as you focus on the top of the stick, and allow your balancing hand to move naturally to make the necessary adjustments, it will stay upright when you let go. As soon as you look away it will fall, so keep your focus. You'll find that very little movement is needed, so don't overcompensate. You might begin charging around the room but you'll soon get the hang of it. As in all circus skills, relax and be confident. If you start with the premise 'this will never work' it probably won't. Surprise yourself – balancing is probably the easiest of circus skills.

Once you can do it on your hand, try it on your chin. Tip your head right back and rest the stick on your chin. It will look as though it's vertical, but it won't be – tip it back a further ten degrees or so. Then all you have to do is focus on the top of it and keep underneath it, just as you did with your hand. It's more difficult, but you can soon get the feel of it. Make sure there's some give in your knees so that you can move smoothly and easily in any direction. If you're ramrod stiff, you haven't a chance! Try it on your foot, elbow, shoulder, knee, nose – anywhere really! If you try it on your foot, try and lift your foot as high as you can because it's easier to focus up than down.

Once you can do those, try it with an unbreakable cup or plate on the top. Put the cup on the stick and find its balance point so that it's steady. Then it's exactly the same – just focus on the bottom of the cup or top of the stick, and gently and smoothly push the stick up until you place it on your chin, finger or wherever. Don't look for the bottom of the stick – feel your way towards it and when you run out of stick you've found it! Then bring on the tray of champagne and . . .

Once you've got the knack and the confidence, find ways of doing it as clowns. Maybe you seem to have no control over the stick or whatever it is that you are balancing. Maybe there's water in the cup that somehow or other ends up falling on your head – your's not somebody else's! Maybe you do a running gag, failing miserably to balance the cup despite any number of sensible methods. But then on the final entrance you appear to achieve it, celebrate joyfully, and take a flamboyant bow, only to give away the secret in the process that the cup is actually nailed on (you've swapped it, of course – you just need an identical stick and cup backstage).

As with all performing, it's the way you do it that makes the difference. As with all skills, you need to be able to do it well in order to look as though you can't do it at all.

In church you could balance the collection plate on the churchwarden's staff, but only if you've checked that the plate is flat-bottomed and not bubbly, and that the congregation will enter into the fun. If it works it's a novel way of offering up the gifts. If you have a procession into church, why not act as servers and balance the candlesticks on your chins – without spraying wax on the congregation. You could try doing intercessions lifting up symbols of the things and people you're praying for, keeping them there in precarious and prayerful balance, halfway between heaven and earth.

There are all sorts of possibilities, but with all balancing, keep your focus, relax, and don't be distracted.

## Banners

Banners are bright and colourful and can say a lot with few words – just like clowns! Use all sorts of materials to make collages and banners, either sewing, sticking or glueing. They don't have to last for ever, so sticking, even pinning would do. They can be designed to walk with and wave, or simply to hang. Use a circus theme – lions for the story of Daniel or the need for courage; the strongman for Samson; a ringmaster for welcome or the need for order midst the chaos; a tightrope walker for the narrow path; elephants for forgetting and forgiveness, or perhaps an elephant and a mouse for Elijah's discovery of God being in the still small voice not the great earthquake or mighty wind. Or do a series of clowns – harlequin, tramp, auguste, jester, whiteface and pierrot were a set we made at Tooting. Each portrays a different emotion and style, or maybe each could carry a different symbol of the gifts of the Spirit. Perhaps a seventh banner would be one with lots of clown faces made and signed by each adult/child, and 'Here we are, fools for Christ's sake' might be the theme. Once you start thinking about it there are infinite possibilities.

## Behave yourself!

This may seem a strange instruction but it does apply, especially in hospitals and hospices where both staff and residents or patients may not exactly be feeling in tune with clowns or fools. Be graceful enough to ask for help and advice before planning a visit or responding to an invitation. Check out what is expected, allowed, encouraged. I can remember some youth club members who nearly killed a pensioner whose room they were decorating by their unwittingly crass behaviour. It was my fault, I hadn't briefed them properly.

We are there as honoured guests and if someone in charge or authority judges it better that we leave, then that's their right, their best judgment for the health of their patients or residents. I remember reading about Ken Feit who in a home for lepers in India wandered about, playing his harmonica, played with puppets and paper animals quietly and gently. No big production. He felt quite useless but was reassured by the staff that he was helping healing to happen. Being there may be much more important than anything we actually do. Go boldly but go gently, gracefully.

## The Bible . . . a barrel of laughs?

Well, yes but you have to go looking with the eyes of a clown. Take the Book of Jonah. To some readers, determined to stop enjoying themselves, this is a terrible cautionary tale about the dangers of not doing what God wants done immediately and the perils that await those who don't jump to it and rush to convert all of Greater London or Manchester.

And it may be precisely that, but there are plenty of jokes along the way. I always imagine Jonah as the sort of person who never does today what he can put off until tomorrow. I know the feeling. So, confronted with the command to convert the people of Nineveh to belief in God, Jonah rushes to the harbour and buys a ticket for a ship sailing as far as possible in the opposite direction. He doesn't realise that God is God of all creation and that wherever you go, God is there too, probably sailing in the first class accommodation!

A great storm blows up, the ship looks in terrible danger of sinking and the crew suspect that Jonah has something to do with it. Jonah confronted by terrified and superstitious sailors admits that he's running away from God and suggests that the sailors might save themselves if they throw him overboard. This they do, gratefully. Along comes a whale, swallows him whole and Joah spends a fishy three days before being spewed up on the beach and trudging off to convert the people of Nineveh.

Jonah the reluctant prophet is a comic character who could have saved himself a lot of trouble by doing God's will in the first place. But the Bible would have been less fun if he had. With the eyes of faith and fun, Bible characters and situations can come alive again, and sometimes for the first time ever.

Other funny stories involve Balaam's incredible talking donkey in the book of Numbers, a donkey rather more perceptive than its prophet rider; Peter's attempt to walk on water which went very well until he began to worry about the wind and the waves; there's the irony of Jesus' mates arguing about who would be the greatest in the kingdom of heaven as they walked towards Jerusalem where Jesus had said he would be killed . . . talk about missing the point! St Paul is not generally thought of as a comic genius but his picture of the parts of the body singing, in effect, 'I get along very well without you' could bring the sober sided pillars of the church crashing down with shouts of encore if imaginatively staged. Pure pantomime. Camels being threaded through the eye of a needle, the blind leading the blind and falling into ditches: these are comic pictures because they reflect the nonsense of so much contemporary culture.

For the blind, read the economist or the psychiatrist or the academic theologian or the 'experts' endlessly arguing some minor point while the world disintegrates around them.

Once we start reading the Bible with clown's eyes or listening afresh with the ears of a fool, there are great mines of laughter waiting to be discovered. And we're offering a prize for the best joke from the book of Leviticus!

## Bubbles

There's something magical about bubbles – I don't know what it is. You can buy kits that make enormous bubbles, machines that churn out hundreds at a time, or just a little pot with the traditional blower. It is a playful thing to do that takes adults back to their childhood and maybe allows them to begin to feel like children again, even children of God.

Bubbles are a tremendously powerful focus for intercessions. Introduce the bubbles by saying something like 'these are such foolish things, so fleeting, so ephemeral . . . and yet so precious. There's something about them. Full of the colours of the rainbow, they remind us of the covenant and promises of God. So let these foolish bubbles be vehicles of our prayers. Our prayers are so foolish in the world's terms, so fleeting, soon forgotten – by us though not by God. They're precious. And as each bubble bursts, know that your prayers are heard.'

Then offer a simple intercession, let the bubbles float and burst, and then quietly offer another.

Why not try doing Noah's Ark with Noah as the clown bubble-blower, full of foolish dreams and notions of boats and floods, who then builds a ludicrously large boat? A laughing-stock to all, yet he proves his as well as God's wisdom, and the bubbles turn out to reflect the sign of God's covenant with mankind. There is also plenty of scope in the story for crazy animals, playing with water, and whitefaces drowning to rapturous applause!

## Build a mad machine

This is a great 'loosen up and get to know you' exercise. I was working with a church group in Milton Keynes and I asked them to become a combine harvester. They all knew I was mad so they had a go. It was a wonder to behold and to hear. They'll never forget the experience. They could just as easily have become a food processing factory, a radio station, television studio or a Churchill tank. And if they ask you 'what's the point?', chances are they've missed it. (Actually it's about playing, playfulness, mad ideas, lateral thinking, trust, and above all, not minding looking stupid and behaving like a bunch of fools! Okay?)

## Danger – gimmicks ahead!

Beware of gimmicks and gimmickry.
The idea of holy foolishness is not that of a barely thought out import from the United States, though we are always ready to acknowledge our debt to holy fools 'over there'.
Holy fooling is hard work, committed work and often very costly in terms of time and effort. For that and other reasons, what we do as holy fools needs thinking and praying through.
We need to know why we're putting on slap, getting into outrageous or bizarre costumes, and taking liberties with those we may meet. It's not for our sake, but God's sake and the Gospel's sake that we do what we do, are what we are.
Foolishness is not some 'cure-all' tool of evangelism that will set the population on fire for God.
It's a work, a ministry to which some feel called.

## Children – don't scare them!

The late Gerald Priestland confessed to having been frightened by a clown at Bertram Mills' Circus at the age of four and to having detested them ever since. Young minds are very impressionable and childhood memories can profoundly affect adult attitudes. Adults, because they look as tall as buildings to very young eyes, can be frightening. And when the adult is wearing very odd clothes and doing strange things, clowns have all the potential to scare children half to death. Add a deathly white face, a loud instrument or two, and disaster threatens the clown's first encounter with the child.

The first tip for clowns working with both children and adults, for adults can just as easily be upset by clowns, is to respect their space. Keep a safe distance from the child, so that the child has space to step back, turn round and withdraw without feeling oppressed. The second tip is to get down to the child's eye-line. Become less scary by making yourself the same height. Bungalows are not as frightening as tower blocks!

The same principle applies to children or adults in bed in hospital. I visited a colleague recently who told me that a doctor had come to visit him in the hospital ward. The doctor had knelt on the floor while visiting. It brought the doctor into proper non-threatening eye contact with the patient while the kneeling also suggested the visitor wouldn't stay over long!

When working with small children be careful not to make exaggerated, and therefore potentially threatening gestures. Clowns exaggerate of course but the smaller the child the larger the exaggerated movement will appear and the greater the chance of frightening the child.

The further away you get from the child, the taller you can more safely become and the more like a silly adult you will become again.

## Christingle themes

The Children's Society distributes resource materials for this traditional service usually held in the few weeks before Christmas. Local groups have organised adults or children to explain where the Christingle came from, and what the various parts of the Christingle mean. The orange is the world, the red ribbon round the orange is the blood of Christ by which we are saved, the fruits on cocktail or orange sticks represent the four seasons with their fruits, and the lighted candle signifies the light of the world, Jesus Christ.

All the available literature stresses the importance of careful adult supervision where children and the lighted Christingles are concerned, the importance of fire precautions, the need for a close watch on what happens to both the candles and small children. If clowns are involved, then extra care must be taken for even the most careful child could forget what he or she is holding in the excitement. I recommend keeping clowning and fooling completely separate from the lighting, distribution and holding of lit Christingles.

A routine that has worked very well when I've used it at a Christingle service is that of the mock auction of a child. This may sound outlandish and slightly shocking, but it can powerfully demontrate just how valuable each and everyone of us is in the sight of God, and therefore I hope, in the sight of one another. Given the perennial scenes of children and suffering at home and overseas, this is a worthwhile lesson.

With a bit of pre-service liaison, I usually arrange for one of the children present to be prepared to volunteer to come and sit on a high stool in front of the congregation. I then ask people to say just how much they think he or she is worth. Adults will generally bid up if the children suggest too low a price. There's plenty of room for pointed observations on the size of cars that local people drive, the central heating, the double glazing that characterise a wealthy neighbourhood, or the roaring trade done by local pubs at Christmas time. I usually sense a real pantomime feel about the congregation's participation in all of this. Plenty of 'Oooh no he isn't . . . ooh yes he is.'

The aim is to demonstrate that there isn't enough money in all the world, not enough Smarties in the clown's bag, not enough money in the collection plate, not enough jewellery in all that town, not enough gold in the bank around the corner to pay what this (and therefore, every) child is worth. In fact this child is infinitely precious, so much so that another small child many years ago grew up and eventually died to show how much each and every one of us is worth.

Another possible Christingle approach is to turn a Christingle nightmare into a Christingle dream come true. Simply contrive for there not to be enough Christingles to go round. One short is quite sufficient. (To avoid disaster it may be important to prime the last child in the queue not to get in a state because we've run out of Christingles just as we get to him.) Then the clowns set out to solve the problem: with enormous scissors they can maybe cut someone's hair ribbon up (no?) or they can try and order tickets for a trip to wherever oranges come from, chop trees down to get some wood to cut into the toothpicks or orange sticks (maybe they come from orange trees too!). There's a fabulously realistic looking saw which makes the most lifelike saw noises, without actually cutting into altars or pulpits, and this could be used to great effect slicing parts of the church up to make some cocktail sticks.

You guessed it, the ultimate and best solution is for the suggestion to come naturally from the children or the adults (preferably the children) that either one could give up his or her Christingle, an act of self-giving love, or maybe one could be conjured out of contributions from those who already have their Christingles: so maybe one does without a stick with the fruits on, another happily lets his orange be cut in half, (after all, most of the time we only see half the world at a time, if that), and a bit of ribbon might be found or we could borrow a mum's lipstick and paint the red band. If half a candle is produced by cutting a candle in two, remember to extinguish it before dividing it. This could be a smashing lesson in sharing gifts, sharing good news, sharing God's love. He does . . . why can't we?

## Christmas themes

The challenge of Christmas is that everyone knows the story – or thinks they do. So tease out the most important part for you, and then find a way of telling it with enthusiasm. Clowns make very good shepherds, rustic types who may be terrified of angel choirs.They might like to try singing along with the angels to the point where the angel can barely get his message across. Shepherds trying to sing the Hallelujah Chorus again and again and the angel has to get quite stroppy and interrupt and say 'Will you listen for a moment'.

Clowns wondering as they go to worship the child suddenly realise they don't know how to worship. What should they do? Panic? Ask the vicar, the congregation? How can they show the little baby that they love him? Give a gift . . . perhaps a bell from round the neck of one of their sheep . . . a lamb, but what would the little family do with a lamb . . . maybe a bell after all . . . it makes a good sound . . . lets people know the sheep . . . err, well, lamb of God is near? And what about the gift of simply listening, or loving and caring for the child in whatever way they can, and isn't that something each of us can do?

Maybe worship could be just going and sharing in the happiness of Mary and Joseph and the miracle of a birth, for isn't God present at every child's birth? Where love is, there is God.

Could clown/shepherds be talking about it a day or two after it happened, what they really thought when the angels brought them the good news and who's going to give that good news to others now the angels have stopped singing and gone back to heaven. Who if not us clowns/shepherds and you lot come to church today . . . and who said 'Yes, but what is the good news?', leading to improvised drawing out of those present just what is the message of Christmas for them and what difference it makes.

And if all this reads as if it's come out of a muddlehead in a few minutes, well it has, and you could do much better.

Maybe the innkeeper and his wife could wonder aloud about the events around the birth while washing up . . . was this tiny child going to make any difference to their everyday lives? Would he help kick out the Romans . . . could he change their lives? This was the Messiah . . . the anointed one . . . could he influence the bloodthirsty king, reduce the taxes, make crooks go straight, heal the sick, cheer up the depressed (God knows there are a lot of them about . . . look at this lot here . . . call yourselves joyful . . . eh?!)? Who are the people who need to hear good news today and tomorrow and next week, and how could we all help that to happen?

## Clown

C is for Clown – how could we not have this one?! But it's Clown with a capital C because Clowns are so important. We need their laughter and their playfulness, their perspective and their nonconformity, their comedy and their tragedy. Both society and the church need Clowns for their sanity and survival. Don't write off Clowns with a capital C – they're not just for kids. They're for you and me . . .

## Clown bands

Brass instruments, bugles, hunting horns, trombones all have their comic uses. For economy there's nothing to beat the humble kazoo or the comb and tissue paper. Recorders, swanee whistles, duck calls, quail calls (very useful when discussing the children of Israel with their diet of manna for breakfast and quails for supper) can all contribute to clowning and foolery. Percussion instruments, drums, tambourines, bongoes, castanets, the humble triangle are great for punctuating speeches, especially the pompous kind.

Instruments, like most accessories, should be used in moderation. That may sound a little 'killjoy was here'-like, but unless a particular instrument is learned and used as a major prop, instruments work best in a sparing supporting role. A clown band should, as far as possible, be well rehearsed otherwise it will sound awful. Put it another way, it ought to be possible to recognise the tune, and wrong notes should be tastefully and intentionally played. Bad musicianship as a joke is extremely short-lived. I should know!

## Clown biscuits

Either as a workshop activity or just for fun refreshments, make clown biscuits. Any simple biscuit recipe will do, and just add a clown face with some piped icing, with perhaps a fancy ruff to finish it off. Or use half a glacé cherry for a nose, currants for eyes, angelica etc. for face designs, and a trimmed cherry or icing for mouth. You could adapt a gingerbreadman recipe and design to make a clown with big boots and a hat, and then add the icing for face and costume. They make good Easter presents for an Easter feast. Why not ice an Easter cake too? Make a clown face with crosses for eyes and a huge smile, maybe an alpha and an omega on the cheeks, and then offer your Easter congregation a slice each and a souvenir biscuit to take home.

## Clown car

There is a great tradition in the circus of clown cars that explode and all sorts of bits fall off. You won't be able to make one of those, but you could make one with cardboard boxes, paint it up, see how many of you can travel in it, and still let various pieces fall off with accompanying noises and puffs of flour/talc instead of smoke. Build up a routine by hiding all manner of unlikely objects in the bonnet which prove to be the cause of the car's undoing – all can be pulled out with a mixture of bravado and puzzlement. Practise falls so that you can be run over or fall off the back. If you can get hold of some funwheels, you can become a proper vehicle. If it's a holiday club, the groups could have a competition for the best car and finish with a very foolish grand prix!

## Collages

Collages are fun because lots of people of differing ages and abilities can do one together, working at their own pace and level. Rather like the banners, use all sorts of materials, though tissue, felt and paper are the most popular. Use junk, wool and cloth – anything really! Circus scenes are fun to do with lots of small scenarios. Collages of troupes of clowns give people the opportunity to contribute a clown of their own. A simple opening activity or even registration for a clown day would be to get each entrant to design a clown face on a large round sticker, sign it, name it, and then put them all together on a great collage of faces. You could add cartoon hats and bodies once they're on!

A harlequin is a more intricate project, with his variegated costume all diamond-shaped, and a half-masked face. Use small shapes or symbols to form the large letters of a word, so Good Friday might be spelt in crosses, Advent in tears, Christmas in cribs and angels' wings, Easter in smiles, pilgrimage in clown boots – draw the outline of the letters in pencil and then stick the designs on. Use clowns in different positions and postures to form the letters of longer words, or give the letters themselves clown boots or hats or bow ties. Create the traditional tragi-comic masks to say something about crucifixion and resurrection, using materials that suit the mood of each mask. You could add a crown of thorns to the tragic mask and a clown hat to the comic one. Talking of hats, why not try a collage of different hats all being thrown up in the air in celebration above the word 'Hallelujah', or above a symbol of Easter or Christmas.

Once you've got a collage that's big enough, why not use it as an altar frontal the next Sunday, or surround the font? Use it appropriately and let everyone get pleasure out of it. Collective efforts are always worth seeing and showing.

## Conviction counts

No communication without conviction. If the message is tired, boring, lifeless and dull, don't bother trying to share it with anyone. This may sound so self-evidently true but sometimes you wouldn't think so. I'm not arguing for frothy enthusiasm painted on faces from an aerosol marked 'INSTANT GLEE, CFC FREE', but somewhere between average gloom and false glee an enthusiastic balance has to be struck.

Clowns frequently exaggerate their actions, their words. Our clownish clothes are over the top, exaggerated, larger than life. And so often in church joy is underplayed, celebration is muted and the watchword seems to be 'Stop enjoying yourselves, this is the house of a very gloomy, joyless God'.

The trouble is, conviction only comes from experiencing the truth of a message myself. If I don't believe in a loving, forgiving, joyous creator God, I'll never be able to convince anyone else. So the watchword is, never try and teach anyone anything you don't already believe in your head and know in your guts to be true. That way, hypocrisy and dishonesty can be kept at bay.

A useful hint may be to get a friend to assess something you do and see if they feel it rings true. If it does, fine. Go out and celebrate. If it doesn't, enlist their help to discover the cause. Are you feeling so tired that your attempts at communicating joy were about as convincing as a second-hand suet pudding masquerading as an award-winning dish in a cookery competition? If so, don't try and communicate life if you're feeling half dead. Get someone else, a fellow fool to rescue you from feeling dead with their liveliness and joy. After all, it's supposed to be infectious. Maybe you're using the wrong kind of language without fully understanding it yourself. And if you don't, what chance have they got? Maybe the material is inappropriate: it's something a friend has suggested which is right for them, where they are on their journey, but wrong for you. If it's wrong for you, you won't be able to share it with anyone else. You'll sound and look like a soup salesman who desperately tries to sell a soup to others which makes him shatteringly sick.

*(See also* **K.I.S.S.***)*

## Costume ideas

Costume and clown character are inseparable. When I try on a hat, any hat, I feel different in some strange way. The hat becomes part of me, or an extension of who I am. That's probably why in the clown 'business' if you hurt my hat, I am likely to feel mortally wounded or at the very least extremely offended. This is no different from the half truth behind those car stickers which read 'You toucha my car, I smasha your face!'. Returning to hats for a moment, the bowler hats or Derbys were part of Laurel and Hardy. I can't think of them without their hats. That's how close costume is to wearer.

Is your character tidy, careful, precise, fastidious about dress? Then that will be reflected in smart, sharp dress, nothing out of place, every item carefully coordinated . . . and

a pointer towards a whiteface clown. Someone who is haughty, clever, perhaps pompous, someone to whom a seagull dropping on his shoulder would be the worst possible insult, the greatest disaster imaginable, an assault on his very self.

Is your character a shambling, muddled, simpleton for whom to remember to get up in the morning is a daily miracle of cataclysmic significance? Then the state of your costume will appear to be largely a matter of chance. To fit in with your character, there will be evidence of forgetfulness less sculpted than thrown together, elements back to front or worn upside down. You will look like a fashion designer's worst nightmare. Colours will clash rather than gently complement one another. Dress or suit will barely fit. There may be room for the rest of the world's population inside any coat or jacket. You are beginning to look like an auguste.

It's difficult to say whether character makes the costume or costume forms the clown's character. They are indissolubly linked. Advertisers peddle the powerful myth that if I buy that suit, this dress, then everything else that I could possibly desire, fame, fortune, attentive colleagues and friends, even success will be added to me. And you will have noted that life isn't exactly like that. And in the whole area of myths about clothes and accessories lies a rich vein for clowns to explore.

One of the most important considerations relating to costume is that of comfort. The clown must be at home within his costume otherwise the discomfort will issue in ways which will affect performance and audience perception. Unless you want your clown to major on being ill at ease in costume, go for costume which is both comfortable and easy to maintain in good clean and fresh condition. I have a marvellous tail coat which is great if I'm a clown waiter precariously balancing six main courses on my left arm while serving at a prison chaplains' annual conference dinner. But it is wildly impractical for most other applications.

Charity shops and jumble and nearly new sales are a rich mine for possible costume elements. Don't be tempted to splash out on something expensively new and tailored until you are quite certain it fits with who you and your clown are. Early in your clown's life, while the character is emerging, there may be a number of costume stages and changes to experience and explore. Don't be surprised at this. Some clothes look great, feel right but simply don't work. They somehow clash with what your clown does, how he or she behaves. If you're not sure, find a friend and get help and advice. You may be the last to see that something isn't quite right and doesn't work.

On the other hand, don't be surprised if something you least expected to work manages to convey a message you hadn't intended but which helps your clown. For example, you may indeed be the fastidious whiteface who majors on appearance but there's always some article of clothing or costume which jars and can be exploited for all it's worth. Fine, but beware of milking one joke until it turns into old cheese.

## Crosses and kisses

An 'x' has three major meanings. An 'x' in an exercise book means that you've got something wrong, it's probably in red and it's pretty unforgiving. Clowns aren't like that nor do they judge people like that – nothing is ever completely wrong because there is always something right or another way of looking at it. Clowns deal in ticks rather than those kind of crosses.

An 'x' could be a multiplication sign, and clowns love to multiply even if the end result isn't quite what it should be. A problem can always be multiplied because then it's more fun to tackle, and a blessing can always be multiplied because blessings are like that if you allow them to be. Multiplication means more, and clowns always want more.

An 'x' could be a kiss too, and while clowns might be hugely embarrassed by kisses, all that they do comes with love, and if real kisses don't seem appropriate then blown ones will do!

Clowns could do a sketch that showed all this, with a large 'x' behind them. Then as they all troop off, one of them hoists the 'x' onto his shoulder and trails off. It's up to you whether you spell out the connections between 'x' and the cross and the love that both denote, but Jesus had to spell it out so sometimes we have to too.

## Diabolo

The diabolo is a fairly simple circus skill, but like all of them there's a knack! It's an old victorian children's toy, so it's not that difficult to master the basics. Shaped like an hourglass, you spin it like a top, and then do all sorts of tricks with it while it's spinning, such as tossing it in the air (and catching it!), rolling it up and down the string, bouncing it, making it jump over your foot, making a cat's cradle – there are books around on the subject if you want to pursue it further.

Basically, you place the diabolo over the string on the floor, and then everything is done with the right hand (or left, if you're left-handed!). Start the diabolo rolling across the floor from right to left and once it is moving, lift up the string so that the diabolo is suspended in the air but turning round. You then have to keep it moving or it will just drop off and it certainly won't do any tricks! You need to get it spinning fast by whipping it – the action is like whisking an egg because it's wristy, small, firm and staccato! Use your right hand to whip and keep the left hand fairly solid and stationary. You want to try to get it spinning as fast as you can.

If the diabolo starts to tilt towards you, push your right hand stick away from you. If it starts to tilt away from you, bring the right hand stick in towards you. You need to try and keep the shape in parallel. Once it's going and isn't tilting, the basic trick is to throw it up in the air and catch it. To throw it up, quickly pull the sticks apart so the string gets taut and the action of that will shoot the diabolo up in the air. If you try to do it with a loose string and hoist both sticks up in the air, it is likely to get tangled. To catch it again, don't just hold the sticks out to dry and hope for the best! Point your righthand stick right at and under the diabolo as it's coming down and the diabolo should roll down the string for you and allow you to recommence whipping. If you want it to jump over your foot, it needs to be going fast enough, but you place your foot on the string to the right of the diabolo and it just hops over for you – if the diabolo is straight and you move your foot away again fast enough.

You can also throw the diabolo to each other – see who can throw it the highest.

It may not need translating but 'diabolo' means devil, and there is plenty of scope for scenes or lessons built around the need to keep the whiphand over the devil so he knows who is his master.

## Drama as worship and vice versa

Worship is theatre, an insight easily neglected. When worship is as unexciting as cold chips, no wonder people die of boredom. They aren't involved, captured by what they see happening. When joyful readings are delivered in the tones of an undertaker on a bad day, worship dies on its knees.

Worship can be light and shade, colour, movement and stillness, silence and noise. Too often there is no quiet, no space in the mad race to say all the words before being beaten by the clock.

Feelings about worship run deep and clowns and fools can gently plumb the depths asking the questions that cry out to be faced. 'What do we think we are doing here?' 'What would happen if we all shut up for a moment and let God get a word in edgeways . . . ?' 'Do we really need so many hymns . . . such long prayers . . . and if the word of God is so important, can't it be read more clearly with some time in which to let it work its way within us?'

Clowns can often bring an overfamiliar bible passage to life again by being thoroughly and rigorously professional in delivering it to the congregation, by asking aloud what it might mean, offering a few answers and suggesting that each of those present needs to work it out for themselves. Clowns can also stand for the notion that there is much more in the scripture and worship than most of us ever dare to believe.

## Easter cards

Cards are always easy to make, but why not make a clown design for Easter? A happy clown face with a smile or gaping laugh is an easy and obvious one, but what about a clown with a daffodil or other spring flowers, or cradling a butterfly (itself a sign of resurrection) in his hands. Draw happy, dancing clowns cavorting round a chosen text. Open the card and let a jack-in-a-box jump out – put 'Surprise, surprise' on the front and have the clown in the box holding a Happy Easter sign. Try a clown with a billboard or sandwich board spelling out your message. Or a clown juggling Easter eggs, or even peering out of one! Or a clown trying to spell Hallelujah on a blackboard on the front of the card – on the inside he's given up and written Hurray! You could use the biblical text, 'The foolishness of God is wiser than human wisdom' as part of the card. I think people would get the message – it would certainly make them think. It partly reflects the possibility that the empty tomb echoed with the sound of God's laughter.

## Eggs

There is a long tradition that working clowns register their faces, their make-up, on eggs. It's a kind of copyright that ensures that no two clowns are exactly the same. Clowns International have re-established the tradition and there is a fine collection of eggs at the Clowns' church at Holy Trinity, Dalston, in East London. You could make your own egg or even start your own collection.

If you want your egg to last a long time, you'll need to blow it. Otherwise you can use a hardboiled one. Then you simply design your own clown face. You can use felt tips, paint or crayons, and add bits of glitter or shapes made from paper. Use wool for hair, or make a tiny hat. Stick on a red nose or a long nose. Use scraps of material to make a miniature costume around the eggcup or stand that it's on, so that it's like a bust with head and shoulders. And give him/her a name! Why not make one of each type of clown that you find in this book?

Eggs are favourite for messy routines too. Trick eggs can be made by filling a blown egg with confetti or water. Use a stone or china egg, throw it up in the air and catch it on a china plate – the plate breaks, not the egg, especially if you scored the plate first with something like a tile-cutter. Nobody wants real eggs all over them – far too messy!

## Emotions

'Smile, you're a clown', shouts the harrassed mother to a less than smiling clown, and yet not all clowns are happy, and no clowns are happy all the time. My favourite definition of the clown is 'the vulnerable lover'. The clown is vulnerable because he is open to all people and possibilities, as well as being prey to all his emotions; and he's a lover because he loves everyone, accepts everyone, wants to play with everyone – but he'll always give you space.

Clowns need to have access to their own emotions in order to communicate them but also so that they know how they feel, never mind what other people feel – a matter of sense and sensitivity.

A simple exercise is for a leader to call out an emotion and everyone else has to communicate that emotion – to the leader, not to anyone else. It's done through the eyes really. You just need to feel a bit of your own happiness and express it, letting your face do it for you – don't grin like a three-year-old posing for a photograph when you're asked to be happy. Then try being sad, proud, angry, beautiful, lonely. Don't try them for long – it's a playful exercise. It's tempting to look at the floor for sadness and loneliness, but we need to look up and have that eye contact. Having gone through each of them a couple of times, encourage people to express it physically too, allowing the body to articulate the emotion – happiness is light and lifted, sadness slumped, anger tense, and so on. Then go through them very quickly, with a snap of the fingers. But try and avoid slipping into remembered poses – it's much better to try to feel a bit of the emotion each time rather than recreating what it was like. Finally, exaggerate each one, both physically and with sound if necessary. Make each one playful so there is a twinkle in the eye. No matter how outrageously exaggerated the emotion, if it is still truthful at its heart it will communicate powerfully.

You could try moving the emotions so that everybody starts by walking sadly, freezes on command, feels some of that sadness, and then moves off again with a different emotion. This whole workshop exercise helps establish the kind of clown you might like to be – tramps are sad and lonely, whitefaces beautiful and proud, auguste happy and clumsy, and so on. But it's also fun for kids.

An alternative workshop for groups of six to ten people is to have sets of two teams working with each other. One team faces the wall and they all turn round together expressing their selected emotion, and the other team have to guess what it is. Or you can play 'In the manner of the word': one person goes out, and the rest have to choose an adverb, like angrily or pompously. The person then comes back into the room and can order any of the players to do any action in the manner of the word, e.g. open the curtains, approach another person, eat breakfast or whatever. The player then opens the curtains pompously, and the person has to try and guess what the adverb is. You keep going with different actions until the word is guessed.

'Crossing the threshold' is another good exercise. Chalk a line or use a plank or scarf or something that would serve to mark where a doorstep might be. Each person then starts by walking towards the 'doorstep' with one emotion, but then the emotion changes in an instant just as they cross the threshold - the change should be obvious both in mood and posture. Using words can help to establish both the emotion and the change, but don't rely on words!

The clown should have the capability and capacity to change his/her mood or emotion in an instant, being playful and yet truthful. It's the basis of clown ministry – the ability to be genuinely sad with the sad, happy with the happy, lonely with the lonely, but also offering the possibility of moving on. You can't minister from a position of invulnerability – it just doesn't work.

## Evangelism and the clown . . . good news or bad?

Clowns are not about pressure. Evangelism of the very worst kind can indeed be about pressure. Consider the doorstep evangelist. The door opens. 'Good morning, Mrs Gutbucket, don't you think the world's in a terrible mess?' (Pressure point 1: only a complete nutcase would answer 'no'.) 'Don't you sometimes wish you could be freed of all the guilt you feel for your part in the terrible mess facing each and everyone of us today?' (Pressure point 2: even if she understood a word he's saying, she's not about to argue unless she has a degree in philosophy.) 'Well, Mrs Gutbucket, by God's grace and some amazing coincidence I have just the answer for your guilt, join our church and it'll all be washed away as quick as a noonday shower.'

Clowns explore questions of faith and belief and commitment with both gentleness and sensitivity. Clowns always honour their hosts with the gifts of space and time to come to their own conclusions. Other people's conclusions, taken in second-hand won't do. Jesus, from what we can see in the gospels, did not believe in clubbing people into the kingdom. Hope may be a good breakfast but fear's a lousy lunch.

Clowns make a point with humour, sensitivity and leave it to God and the listener to work at together. Clowns tell stories, some from the Bible, some from their own experience and let the stories work their own miraculous magic with the listener, the watcher. People are more likely to be convinced by the clown who works with love than by the evangelist who works with fear wrapped up in frothy patter.

## Exaggeration

Clowns are larger than life. And clowns are everyone. What happens to clowns, the bucket of water, the custard pie, the trips and falls, the banana skin, happens to each one of us. Clowns exaggerate reality to the point where we laugh at the petty things that happen to us which we take to be great disasters. And when we laugh at the clown and the things that clowns experience, we begin to laugh at ourselves and at our experiences, begin to take ourselves less solemnly. And in learning to laugh at ourselves we start to love ourselves a little more, to the point where, free from self-centred anxieties, we can give ourselves away to others. Love God, love your neighbour as yourself (Leviticus 19.18 after extra time). So long as I'm preoccupied with what happens to me, and how downtrodden and upset I am, there is nothing of me worth giving to anyone else even if such a generous thought could find some space to grow inside me.

Exaggeration by the clown helps people to see what is happening. The further away the watcher, the greater the exaggeration needs to be in order to be seen. It's also important for people to understand that what they are seeing is larger than life, is over the top so as not to miss the point that it is a comic portrayal of how life really is.

Costume is a help here. When I put on my huge clown shoes, I have to take large exaggerated steps. When I put on baggy trousers, I become bigger and baggier than I usually am. When clowns go 'over the top', it is almost as if we are stepping into the unknown. Life in the day-to-day ordinary world is usually understated. We are not normally an emotionally demonstrative race. In fact we're probably far too repressed for our own health. Exaggeration draws us towards the possibility of being a bit more up-front, more expressive, more at home with feelings and emotions and all the risks that their expression may bring. Exaggeration is a vital tool in making points that sink in and begin to work, a tool of meaning.

## Facepaints

There's an argument for saying that this should be under G for Greasepaints, because that's what clowns traditionally use and that's what I prefer. Nevertheless, greasepaint is oil-based, a bit messier, and has to be taken off with baby oil; whereas the popular facepaints are water-based and come off with soap and water. Assuming you've chosen whether you want to be an auguste, a whiteface, or a tramp, here's an introduction to those three types.

If you're an Auguste, look at your face in a mirror and make lots of faces so that you can see how your face works, where the lines and dimples are. Your face is unique, just as your clown face will be. Decide which of your features you want to magnify – if you've got a large nose, do you want it to remain a feature by sticking an even bigger red nose on it, or do you want it to be smaller so you put a little red dot on the end? You could put big shapes around the eyes, and

I always recommend eyeliner and mascara to make the eyes work whatever you choose to do around the eyes themselves. Have you got sharp features or round ones, because that will dictate the contours of the shapes that you use on your cheeks, for instance? The face you create should help you to communicate more effectively rather than just being pretty or clever. Most clown faces are symmetrical, so each side of the face complements or reflects the other. Use an eyeliner to trace the shapes you want to use and then colour them in. Start with the lightest colours first. It's worth then accentuating that outside line because it gives the shapes and the face the necessary definition. The golden rule is to keep it simple – don't be too intricate and don't use too many colours. In the end you'll find a face that really is yours and suits you and nobody else.

If you're a european whiteface you need a completely white face – and neck, traditionally. So cover the face first, including all round the eyes and under the chin, so there is no flesh visible. Every whiteface has a distinguishing and distinguished eyebrow, so use a cotton bud to trace an elegant eyebrow, and then fill it in – the cottonbud removes the white and thus stops the colours blending and blurring. Decide if you want a simple design on one cheek, or perhaps a bit of sparkle. Add a little colour to the lips so that they can be seen to be moving, and eyeliner and mascara to the eyes, and you're ready. The British tradition is to redden the ears, but that's optional. The American whiteface is quite different from the European because it is essentially a whiteface base but with auguste features. It can be quite pretty too, and a lot of female clowns use the whiteface base and then add pretty but exaggerated features, not least the huge fluttering eyelashes!

Tramp is a scruffy clown, an old-fashioned hobo. You need a beard, achieved by rubbing in the black – you can choose whether to have a solid black beard or a more stubbled effect. The mouth is usually white. Add some red to the cheeks, perhaps a hint of blue to give it an alcoholic hue, and a nose to match. Bring the eyes down by using an eyeliner under the eyes which then tails off downwards, and you're there. There's an ancient tradition that clowns are neither male nor female, just clowns, so females can have beards if they want! If you're not happy with a beard, create a bag lady in a similarly grubby vein.

You can add a Christian dimension to all of these faces by using Christian symbols as part of the design – crosses on the cheeks, fishes around the eyes, hearts anywhere you like, etc. But they still have to suit your face and character: Christian symbols, like Christian faith itself, should never be gratuitous but rather be very much part of you. If it doesn't fit and isn't right, it's obvious.

Finally, if you have been using greasepaints rather than facepaints, you should powder it. Use talc and a powder puff or lump of cotton wool, and just pat it all over your face. Brush off the excess with a make-up brush or cotton wool, and then spray or pat with water to get rid of the rest. This sets it, protects it, and allows your make-up to look good for much longer.

## Falls

Clowns are renowned for their falls – or at least augustes are! Irrepressible and resilient, they always bounce back. Vulnerable they may be, but they pick themselves up, dust themselves down, and start all over again. There's an india rubber quality about them that helps and ensures their survival.

But if you're going to do falls, make sure that you do them properly and don't hurt yourself at all. Small children think clowns falling over is absolutely hilarious, and good falls bring good laughs. But if you get hurt, it's not funny for you or for anybody else.

Learn to do falls on a crash mat or a mattress or something that will give you a soft landing – no need for masochistic martyrs here! The principle of falling is not to fear it – just let it happen. If you worry, you'll stick a hand out and break your wrist or jar your knee. You need to break the fall but not by using fragile joints – keep your knees, elbows and wrists out of the way. The standard fall is a sort of sideways collapse and you hit the ground along the length of the side of your body, bit by bit from the calf upwards. If it's done smoothly and you keep your elbows and knees out of the way, it's simple, but you've got to collapse like a drunkard or as if you've just been filleted. There's a sense in which you've got to love the floor as it's coming up to greet you and you just sink into its embrace.

Falling backwards is easier than it sounds because you break your fall by almost literally sitting back onto one of your heels as you go back – for a moment you're sitting on one haunch! Then as you go all the way over thrust that foot out again and nobody notices. On the whole, people see where you start and how you end up and don't worry too much about what happens in the middle, as long as it's fast and slick. The only thing to beware is you must keep your head braced upwards so that you don't let it flop back and crack against the floor. Another basic principle for clowns is that as soon as you've gone down, you must come straight back up again, or at least stick your head up and smile to let people know that you're alright. Otherwise people worry for ages afterwards and that's distracting. It's worth practising going backwards but then rocking straight back up to your feet or to a sitting position, using the spine as a fulcrum.

The banana skin fall is similar to the first one except it's quicker. The principle is that as you put one foot down it skids sideways behind your standing foot, and you just follow it down on your side. A fun way to practise it is to be a soldier standing at ease, who as you are called to attention stamps with the salute and the foot disappears as you stamp.

If you want to make the fall seem or at least sound more dramatic, slap the floor as you hit it – sound effects are effective!

The more you fall, the easier it is. If you've got a group of four or five of you, play a game where if you get touched by one of the others you have to fall in the direction that the touch demands. It makes it all the more interesting if the touches are apparently accidental or seem to be quite natural, and the person who touches can't work out what is happening and is bewildered by the consequences –

especially when he promptly goes down the next moment as someone else brushes by. Play it in a confined space and see what happens. If there's an audience, make sure you practise the reassuring looks too.

Another fall that can be funny, and this is a good context to try it, is the delayed fall – rather like the cartoon character who disappears over the edge of the cliff and hovers for a few improbable moments in mid air, sees his plight, and then falls. There are times when it works for clowns too – playing with peoples' expectations and then surprising them or falling into line.

Falls are a basic part of physical comedy and a valuable part of the clown's repertoire and armoury, but don't get too many bruises in the process.

## Feast of Fools – upside-down-ness

The Feast of Fools was celebrated in the medieval church as a safety valve for the pent-up feelings in communities. Roles were reversed and instead of the bishop or abbot being at the top of the hierarchical tree, they became the lowest of the low while their subordinates lorded it over them as lords of misrule, abbots of unreason and princes of fools. Rules were overturned, put into suspension while the feast was enjoyed. The junior clergy could say exactly what they thought of their elders without fear of punishment. Truth and laughter were allowed to pierce pomposity. The words of the Magnificat came to life. The mighty were put down from their seats and the humble and meek were exalted. Jesus washing dirty feet the night before he died pre-figures this role reversal.

Inevitably the church could only stand so much of such mischief and honesty and the tradition was killed off, but then spread throughout secular society. I suspect there is as much, if not more, need for this means of truth-telling today as ever there was within and outside the church. That responsibility can be embraced by fools and clowns who, because we use humour and laughter to cloak what we say and do, may seem less threatening to authority and those who fear for their status.

## Feather dusters

These are marvellous accessories. They can be both badge of office and a means of welcome. Use them for dusting down people as they come into church as part of meeting and greeting. Some people are so used to not being welcomed that it's a joyous surprise. It's only right that we should be dusted off as we come to worship God. But beware, not everyone knows quite how to react to being so dusted. Trust your wits and be prepared to find other ways of meeting and greeting. We were clowning outside Westminster Abbey for Comic Relief one Red Nose Day. Tens of tourist coaches rolled up and parked and we greeted the Italians and the Japanese with feather dusters and collecting buckets. How they explained their photos when they returned home we will never know but it's fun to imagine what they said.

And another thing, don't use your greeting feather duster for real dusting as we don't want holy fools known for bringing on asthma attacks amongst those we're supposed to be welcoming.

## Feet

Feet are terribly important! Clowns are always putting their great big foot in it, and outsize boots remain a classic clown symbol and a wonderful bit of costume. You can make clown boots with papier mache and varnish, building them up from ordinary shoes. Or you can stuff the ends of shoes that are too big for you, or buy plastic outers from the local joke shop. If you go the whole way and buy proper ones, be warned – they're expensive!

Feet are smelly and embarrassing and funny. On Maundy Thursday when we remember the washing of the disciples' feet, we forget how smelly and dirty and funny they are. Some churches re-enact the footwashing as part of their Maundy Thursday service, but most feet are well washed, scented and even gartered beforehand! The auguste clown is the servant clown – servant to whiteface and indeed servant of all. What would he do if given a bowl of water and a towel and a dozen pairs of feet – tickle them? Soak them? Trip over them? No. He'd caress and wash them, putting us and our predictable expectations to shame. But then when he's finished . . . There's that lovely bit where Peter says, 'Not my feet only . . . ' – well, he asked for it, said the clown! But would he do it?

In Holy Week, why not make a huge paper banner in the shape of a boot, maybe with a huge toe sticking out of the end, and then everyone has to take their shoes and socks off, step into trays of paint and leave their footprints on the banner. Perhaps then the leader or minister could be deputed to wash the paint off everybody's feet.

If that's too messy, people could draw around their shoes, and sign their shoeshape, perhaps adding a symbol of their own – make sure all the feet are going the same way and there's a sign of pilgrimage. The banner could be used again on Good Friday to talk about the way we put our foot in it, the mess we make of things, and our need for forgiveness. Or if it's the shoeshape banner, the way that leads to the cross. Perhaps the point is made that God isn't like that huge Monty Python boot that descends from the sky at random to crush us to death – he's walked the path before us and knows where it leads. Then on Easter Day, perhaps the bare feet show holy ground, or it's the road to Emmaus, or the Easter people setting out on the journey of faith.

Oh yes, feet are important – we can't do silly walks or even foolish pilgrimages without them!

## Foolishness

Foolishness is many things: it is truth-telling and its attendant risks. Consider the fate of the Old Testament prophets who told the truth and took the consequence. Foolishness is loyalty that would tie the fool to his master no matter what happened as in ' . . . let him in constancy follow the master.' Foolishness is following Christ's topsy-turvy commands to love our enemies, to turn the other cheek, to lend without thought of return, to give up life in order to find it.

It is to adventure into the unknown, the scary, the dark and sometimes dangerous world of reality where suddenly fantasies don't work any more and friends vanish from sight. But foolishness is to believe there is one who has been through the worst we can do to one another and who is there to strengthen, to encourage and support.

To be foolish is to believe in the healing power of laughter, the strength of stories and the delight of dance. And to be foolish is to rediscover the wonder of the child, the belief that truly in Christ all things are possible and that each of us is loved, accepted and forgiven. In a tough and cynical world what could be more foolish?

## Fun and games

Clowns and fools ought to be inseparable from the excitement and anticipation associated with fun and games. Too many church events are passive. Weddings can become grisly match of the day spectator sports where guests can see nothing more for them to do than comment on hats and the fact that they couldn't hear Emma make her promises.

While clowns and fools may perform, what they do must involve those present at one level or another. Fun and games are ways of finding whether the audience/congregation have died. Better still, they can be the means of others joining in the flights of fancy, imagination, wonder and sheer playfulness characterised by the clown or the fool. Too much solemnity has banished joy from church. Remember Joy – tall thin girl with glasses?

I recall one seminar group becoming in a matter of minutes an amazingly visual car production line. There are books and books full of team games, parachute games, trust games which are enormous fun, carry risks (often the risk of enjoying oneself) and which also carry vital messages to do with relationships, co-operation, enjoyment, possibilities.

Because clowns often make mistakes and survive the collapse of careful plans, they can be excellent guides through the maze of available games. Because we, the clowns, make mistakes, it's alright for others to fall short too. It's not the end of the world. There is always forgiveness, acceptance, resurrection. What matters is that we are prepared to risk, to venture, to step into the dark, the unknown.

There are lots of games around and lots that are deemed to be terribly useful and group dynamical, if there is such a word. But if you've got lots of people of all ages, and especially if you've only got adults, why not revert to those children's games of your youth? Games of 'tag' or 'it' in all their variants are great fun and get people moving. Musical chairs and musical statues are worth a go, even those silly relay races that always appeared so absurd, but my favourite is Grandmother's Footsteps. One person stands at the other end of the room/hall and faces the wall while everybody else tries to creep up on her and touch her on the shoulder. 'She' is allowed to turn round as often as she likes and if she sees anyone moving that person is sent back to the start. Try it singly, but then try doing it as pairs, holding hands – if either of the pair moves, both get sent back. Try fours, try everyone! It's a good exercise for learning the basics of poise and concentration and energy – if you're not all there and are too lackadaisical, you'll always get caught. Clowning demands that energy of performance that means you can respond to anything in a given instant because, contrary to appearance, you are all there!

Clowns invite people to play, and familiar, often fondly remembered games are as good a start as any. 'Let us play!'

## Gravity and gravitas

Gravity is to do with weight, as Isaac Newton discovered, while gravitas has a lot to do with dignity – put the two together and they're a fearsome combination because they force people to take themselves far too seriously. What people who take themselves too seriously don't realise is that you can't take them seriously at all – and it's only the people who take themselves seriously who don't realise it! It's the clown's job to keep reminding people of that before they are too weighed down by the impending gravitas. It's why kings and queens had jesters, and why bishops need fools too. For a bishop to be led into his cathedral church by a clown with a feather duster hoisted high but also with great solemnity reminds him of the nature but also the origin of his authority, as well as the folly of both the task assigned to him and the expectations others have of him. Clowns are the great debunkers who pull down the mighty from their seats and who persuade us to laugh at ourselves and our foolish pretensions and imperfections. In that laughter we suddenly find that we get the joke and can accept ourselves for who and what God made us to be. The apple may have fallen on Isaac Newton's head and led him to 'discover' gravity, but Adam wasn't so lucky – in picking the apple he chose gravitas, and things have never been quite the same since!

## Great clowns

There are good clowns and bad clowns, just as there are good and bad of everything. Sometimes it depends on personal taste and sense of humour as to whether you find a particular clown funny. But there are great clowns too, who are undeniably wonderful at their art. The best way to learn about clowns and clowning, other than trying it for yourself, is to watch the great clowns in action. Some of them are on tapes and television programmes, but they are few and far between. Some still perform today. Catch them if you can –

live performance is what it's really about because the best clowning is of the present moment.

What makes a great clown? There's nothing false or artificial about him. Entirely plausible and full of integrity, great clowns whisk us off into worlds we never even dreamt of – some of their tiniest actions speak volumes. It seems for a sublime time that nothing is impossible or even improbable. They move us to laughter in one moment and tears the next – quite uncontrollably and yet naturally. They may not seem to be masters of their own destiny, yet for a short while at least they are masters of ours!

Opinions vary as to who the greatest clowns have been, but Joey Grimaldi was the first great English clown. He lived two hundred years ago and his was the world of pantomime. He originated the greasepaint that clowns have worn since, and clowns are still nicknamed Joey after him. Grock, born in Switzerland, was a wonderfully inventive and musical clown who played in theatres and music halls for much of his illustrious career. Charlie Chaplin, of course, a lovely tramp clown, was born in England but made his name and home in the USA. His was the world of films, especially the silent era. Coco has become an almost generic name for clowns in the UK, but Coco was Russian-born and became one of the great children's clowns, working in Bertram Mills' Circus for many years. Popov, star of the present Russian Circus, is regarded as one of the greats. Tremendously skilful, he wears a minimum of make-up. Emmett Kelly and Otto Griebling, both tramp clowns, were two of the great American clowns of this century; and Charlie Rivel, Spanish born, and Charlie Cairoli who worked the Blackpool Tower Circus for so many years, were two of the greats in Europe. Add to them troupes like the Fratellinis and the Rastellis and other great clown families, and you find there is a long parade of clowns who have touched the hearts and lives of children and adults alike, and we are grateful for their greatness.

## Harvest ideas

I once took a part in a harvest family service where I thought it was high time the vegetables were allowed their say. I bought a large marrow, hollowed out eyes and a mouth, grafted on a carrot nose and glued on some grass hair. I hid with this marrow in the pulpit before the service started. When the vicar started his sermon, the marrow suddenly appeared and began to discuss with him the place of vegetables in harvest festivals and in everyday life.

Think adventurously! Build the congregation into combine harvesters, engage vegetables in conversation, encourage churchgoers to become vegetables and ask them what they really think about harvest, the inequalities of food distribution in the world, how the church could help third world people to become self-sufficient.

Convene a fruit and vegetable tribunal with creation's witnesses giving evidence against humanity, coming to a verdict and sentence. The court ushers could be the clowns or fools. Imagine baked beans being allowed to have their say . . . as if they don't already!

Organise a re-run of the feeding of the five thousand, or the five hundred or the fifty with the co-operation of every churchgoer, perhaps collecting up contributions and seeing if there's enough to fund a trip to a takeaway or a chip shop.

What does it feel like to be part of an unexpected miracle? And is the fact that we don't expect miracles the reason for there being fewer than we think Jesus promises.

What would the harvest of us look like, feel like? Have we really been caught by more faithful disciples, and what does being caught mean? So you've started thinking in a wild sort of way? Hurrah!

## Hats

Hats are wonderful things because they're so full of character. Sadly hats are less popular in Britain than they used to be – you don't have to wear them to church anymore, and hats don't seem to be terribly stylish, unless you're going racing at Ascot or invited to a smart wedding. Hats are still worn for functional purposes – to keep the rain off, the head warm, or the sun out of your eyes. Sometimes a particular style of hat becomes a fad or even almost obligatory, like the baseball cap that is so compulsory and compulsive in the USA. But what has happened to the individual choice, the hat that speaks volumes of the character beneath it, the hat that says it all? It's not that eccentric to wear a hat, or is it?

One of the most important bits of costume in establishing your own clown character is the bit that goes on your head. It might be a huge red wig, or a tiny topper, or a bald pate with ginger flaps at the side, or an elegant feathery creation – it could be anything, but you know as soon as you've got it when it's right. Somewhere there's a hat or a wig that's yours and you recognise it like a long lost friend.

Hats can be juggled with, balanced on your nose, rolled down your arms and across your shoulders, flipped in the air to land on your head, from either hand or foot. They can be used for collections, as baskets and bags – they can become anything you like with a bit of imagination. They can hide and secrete all manner of objects, whether it's a rabbit, six eggs or your brain cells! Hats are fun to play with.

A way into finding clown character is to have a whole collection of hats, and then encourage people to choose the hat that appeals to them. Once the hat is on, it immediately bestows a certain character on the wearer, and it's the wearer's task to try to find a way of walking and moving that suits the hat. Sometimes there's an obvious way of moving, especially if it's a hat that is usually part of a uniform of some description, but even the most obvious hats can move us in mysterious ways, indeed in ways we'd never even have imagined. Allow the hat to move you rather than dream up some terribly clever way of doing it – clown character is discovered by instinct and experience. Then, as you're walking round, give your character a name, and then an occupation, how you spend your time. Allow that knowledge to occur to you. Then try finishing a sentence such as:

'the thing you ought to know about me is . . . '
'the only trouble with me is . . . '
'the thing I've never told anyone about is . . .'
'the motto I've always lived by is . . . '

In a workshop, get each person in turn to come out in front of all the others and introduce themselves in those terms. Each should come to the middle, stop, look at their audience and thus feed off them, and then finally talk, before disappearing with a farewell and a doff of the hat, if appropriate. You soon discover if the character is either working and plausible and thus worth pursuing, or whether you've put too much thought and cleverness into it and it is thus a bit shallow and unconvincing.

Another hat game is to put a pile of hats in the middle of a circle of people and in turn you grab a hat, strike an appropriate pose, and say something characteristic. The next person can either respond and build up a story or do something quite different. Hat relays can work similarly, where each 'runner' must walk or run in the character of the hat they pick up.

Simple hats can be made as a craft activity – conical hats with pompoms, top hats and wigs (*see* **Wigs!**) – out of card or materials. They provide something to take home as well as the chance to dress up and become a character.

Yes, look for a hat, try one and when you find the right one fling it high in the air – wouldn't 'Alleluias' be great if they were accompanied by a volley of hats being hurled heavenward . . . ?

## Holy Fools UK history

A bishop rang me one day and suggested I should spend a month at St George's House, Windsor on a mid-service clergy course. Great idea, smart address and if it got really boring I could count the planes flying down into Heathrow. There was a catch hidden in the small print. Students had to agree a subject with one of the tutors and research it before writing 10 to 12,000 words before the course began. I agreed to study the Church and Communication and promptly forgot all about it.

Until, that is, students and wives were invited to spend a day at Windsor, meeting the staff and looking round the House. 'How's the project going?' asked Dr John Long. 'It isn't. I've gone off the Church and Communication.' Long deepening silence. 'What about music?' I used to play a twelve string guitar but I didn't read music. A longer, deeper silence. Then I heard myself saying, 'I know, I've always wanted to study the connection between fools, clowns and the gospel.' To my certain knowledge I had never thought that in my life. However, he became as excited as I was and the dance began. I met clowns, people who trained clowns, heard about the clown, mime, puppet, dance and storytelling workshops in the USA. I studied the history of fools and clowns and the whole question of humour and laughter. I also met Roly Bain who was contemplating writing a book about clowns and fools following a well received sermon on 'Christ the Clown' at theological college. He wrote the book *Fools Rush In* (Marshall Pickering, 1993).

We were encouraged to organise a week-long clown, mime, puppet, dance and storytelling workshop at Southlands College on the clear understanding that hundreds of Americans would rush across the Atlantic to join. They didn't. So Roly, Sandra Pollerman, Lala Winckley and a few others set up a weekend workshop at St James's Piccadilly and out of that halting beginning the Holy Fools (UK) were born.

Eleven years later we held our first AGM. We are a very loosely structured body of around two hundred or so men, women and children who in our different ways and at our own pace explore what it means to be foolish in a holy sort of way. Individuals run prayer and clown workshops and clown skills courses. We try to go wherever people are foolish enough to invite us: missions, cathedrals, conferences, prisons, psychiatric hospitals, hospices, schools. We publish *Foolish Times* four times a year as a means of keeping in touch and sharing ideas and insights.

## Holy Week ideas

There is said to be a traditional connection between Good Friday and All Fools Day (April 1st), indeed that the original Good Friday was April 1st and that is why All Fools Day is on that day. Whether that is true or not, it makes sense in that that was the day when Jesus had the last laugh, not on the Romans, nor the Jewish leaders, nor even the disciples, but on death itself. The clown is increasingly becoming seen as a symbol of resurrection as the empty tomb echoes with the sound of laughter. Given that kind of background, clowns are a good theme for Holy Week.

Palm Sunday presents possibilities not only for processions and palms but congas and costumes! How about a clown band to lead it rather than a solitary cornet player who'd rather be eating one than playing one? One of the earliest presentations of the crucifixion had Jesus with an ass's head, and Palm Sunday is the time that an apparent ass rode into Jerusalem on an ass – any fool could see he was signing his own death warrant. Make some ass's ears out of card and staple them to a cardboard band to go round your head. Fix a tail to your trousers. Have someone in clown costume riding piggyback, and let everyone cheer. Or go the whole hog, to mix animals and metaphors, and make a pantomime horse or donkey, so there are two of you inside the beast. In a workshop or holiday club have a complete donkey derby and let the cheering hit the roof, but then when it comes to Good Friday, the clown takes the donkey's ears and it is boos that he hears as the hosannas turn to shouts of 'Crucify'. Adapt the old parlour game of putting the tail on the donkey, so that everyone puts their own tail on the clown so he carries all to the cross, each one a painful lash and terrible reminder of the games people play.

If you can borrow a real donkey for a Palm Sunday procession, it's usually wise to leave it tethered outside the church during the service. Church carpets can cost a fortune to clean. If you can't get hold of a real donkey, it might be worth trying to find a pantomime horse costume and converting it to a donkey with longer ears and a long tail. I once spent three hours inside such a costume and had to be revived with neat whisky. Don't attempt to carry Jesus on the back of a pantomime horse. You won't be able to afford the surgeon to repair those inside. Seriously, though, a donkey, real or pantomime, can make useful points with the aid of some clowns or fools. Christians are called to be Christ-bearers, and that means that we are sometimes led where we don't want to go, seem foolish in the extreme, and may have developed our long ears through trying hard to hear God's whispering voice.

Explore the foolishness of the events of Holy Week by taking the characters of Holy Week and decide which kind of clown each might have been: Peter the auguste, ever willing and simple but always getting it wrong; Judas the Tramp, the unacceptable outsider, condemned to isolation; Caiaphas and his cronies as whitefaces who took themselves far too seriously but eventually got their comeuppance. What was Jesus? Dress people up as each of the characters and put them on trial – the punishment is a custard pie if they're found guilty of human folly, but that can be compared with the wisdom and the wonder of the divine folly of Jesus, and the foolishness of God that is wiser than our wisdom. Costumes can be simple – just a hat would do: a crash helmet for Peter? Blinkers for Judas? Mitres for the high priests? The traditional Whiteface hat is a short conical hat – these could be replaced by the longer dunce's hat on the passing of judgement.

Maundy Thursday gives the chance for a Feast of Fools, a bizarre banquet. Make silly foods and clown biscuits, design wonderful menus, have the pudding first and the starter last so that everything is turned upside-down. Have waiters spinning plates and doing acrobatics and manipulation with them, juggling the cutlery, and threatening diners with custard pies. And in the midst of the madness find the moment of reverence that recognises the breaking of the bread and the presence of Jesus. Have an after-dinner speaker who preaches not a solemn sermon but a witty word, and a cabaret that performs and proclaims it. *(See also* **Feet**.*)*

On Good Friday, make papier mâché masks like the traditional comedy and tragedy masks – one representing the crucifixion, the other the resurrection. Make a banner incorporating the design. Get everyone to make a happy clown mask and mount it on a cross made from thin garden canes so that it can be carried like a ball mask – then the point can be made that the smile of joy on the front is only made possible by the cross that supports it – comedy and tragedy, death and resurrection are inseparable.

Make an altar frontal or wall hanging with a crown of thorns for Good Friday and a jester's cap and bells for Easter – the truth-teller is revealed in all his glory. How about an Easter Garden with clown figures – perhaps even the empty tomb as the gaping laugh of a clown's face, the red nose the stone that was rolled away?

## Improvisation

There's a long piece of string connecting improvisation and a totally scripted presentation. Because I have difficulty in memorising lines, I prefer to improvise and that's sudden death to any scripted routine. I can't make up my mind if the fault is a memory already full to overflowing with irrelevancies, the gross registered tonnage of the first ship I worked on as a radio operator, the average thickness of electrical transformer laminations, or whether I am genetically incapable of memorising chunks of script.

I greatly admire those who have the gift of an orderly memory but I have stopped envying them. I find the freedom and scariness of improvisation extremely heady, and at least if my words aren't working, I haven't a whole script to throw away. The danger is to think that improvisation does not need careful preparation. All performance does and the audience or congregation has a right to expect it from us.

Many performers find freedom within the discipline of learned lines and I'm glad for them. I don't, for the reasons set out earlier, and for me there's the compensating buzz of the absolutely unknown. My guess is that improvisation is closely related to the practice of playing with words, with a playful approach to situations and a conviction that 'why not?' is a healthier question to ask than 'why?'

## Indestructibility or resurrection

It is a circus tradition that whatever happens to clowns, a bucket of whitewash in the face, a plank colliding with someone's backside, an exploding car or a collapsing ladder, the clown always rises again, gets up and continues. For this reason, clowns are rightly seen as resurrection figures. The worst tragedy in the circus is for a clown to really die in the circus ring.

If clowns and fools are icons, images of the risen Jesus, then we have to become the poor who make many rich, the dying who give life to others, the sad who bring joy and laughter, the vulnerable lover who may not get the girl but who knows it's worth the risk, the beaten down but not counted out. A wise bishop once remarked that the resurrection of Jesus means nothing if we don't experience it for ourselves in the commonplace, the day to day.

So don't sell out. Don't write sketches in which resurrection is denied. In the story of the clown of God, yes the old clown dies . . . but not before his last juggling has brought joy to the sombre faced Christ child. Holy fools and clowns share the calling to be resurrection people, and in so being, remind others that the call is to them too.

## Innocence?

The age of innocence is past. Things are not what they were. Touch a child at your peril. Clowns and children may once have been able to play happily together in innocence. Not now. Sadly, contact is dangerous because of suspicions of child molesting . . . so it's

probably wise not to sit a child on your knee, not to be left alone with a child, and to be extremely careful that any behaviour is not liable to misunderstanding.

This does not mean, thank God, that clowns and fools and children should not meet and enjoy one another's company. Or not, as was illustrated the other day at a Christingle service when a four- or five-year-old decided he didn't like my jester character and said he'd punch me on the nose. Ah, sweet innocence of youth! Did I consider suing him for verbal assault? Of course not . . . I might have said the same in his shoes!

## Innocent as doves?

Innocence is a quality I admire in children. And before you jump up and say, 'you should see my children, right little devils they are!' I would add that all the time I visited village primary schools I wondered what it was that turned innocent children into world-weary cynical adults: the exam system, life, their families, their friends? I never found a satisfactory answer.

In politics and other areas of life innocence and simplicity are despised, written off as simply inappropriate ways of being. I disagree. There is an innocence, a simplicity which is worth its weight precisely because it calls into question the way life is, the way decisions are made, the way things happen, the crazy assumptions which underpin our world: money matters more than people; I'm more important than you, worth more than you; status, possessions are everything; buy this and you'll be successful; drive this car and you can be in heaven too. What nonsense!

Clowns and fools, especially holy fools, have the chance, perhaps even the calling to question these nonsenses. Call me naïve, innocent . . . I'll take it as a compliment.

## Invention and imagination

There is no one or right way to be a clown or a fool. There is the way you find right for you and those with whom you engage. But important ingredients in the mixture or recipe are invention and imagination. They are closely related. I suspect they arise out of a determination that what we see or hear or think isn't God's last word on the matter, so why should they be ours?

Children demonstrate this faculty for inventiveness. A cardboard box becomes a fort, a car, a Sherman tank, a mad ambulance or racing car. A length of hosepipe, some fittings and a small post horn can become an enormous stethoscope. A portable lectern became a mirthshaking failed holy deckchair when I was offered it as a sort of moveable pulpit. A bugle can become a speaking trumpet, a trombone a magical adjustable hearing aid. In the same way a stable became a delivery suite, a kingly throne room, a couple of planks on a rubbish tip the scene of our salvation.

If God's word is true that everything is possible to those with faith, then clowns and fools are in a good position to exemplify and prove this to be the rule rather than the exception. A dim, gloomy church becomes the setting for joy and excitement, a dead congregation the temple of God's Holy Spirit.

## Inversion of status

One of the wonderful things about the clown is that for him all people are equal, and are to be treated equally. It doesn't matter whether it's a baby, a businessman or a bishop. The clown doesn't stand on ceremony or recognise status but simply turns everything upside down in order to check it's the right way up. It's this upside-downness that's worth exploring – it's difficult walking across the room on your hands but you could try holding a conversation between you doing headstands! Why not put a young girl in the chair at your next church meeting and see what that does to the agenda? Or make a boy churchwarden for the Sunday, sitting in the special seat, directing people up for the Communion which he isn't entitled to? Send the minister to the creche so that you can listen to the children and let the minister be seen but not heard. Put the congregation in robes and the clergy and choir in civvies. Or turn everything round in church for a day – if the pews are fixed, would people dare to turn round? Now there's a new slant on repentance.

For the clown everyone is a VIP and nothing and everything is sacred.

## The jester

The jester was the traditional court fool and his great privilege and art was that he was the truth-teller, the only one who was allowed to speak the truth to the king. If he did it with humour he would get away with it, if he didn't get it right he could lose his head. Being a jester was a risky business! The story is told of one jester, a great favourite of the king, who got it wrong, was banished from the land, and warned that if he ever set foot on English soil again his head would be severed from his body. A week later he returned to the court to the general astonishment of all, and when challenged by the king that he had been told never to set foot on English soil again, simply took off one of his shoes and poured out a fair quantity of earth onto the floor. 'Sire', he said, 'I stand on French soil!' He was pardoned forthwith.

Jesters play with words as well as people and remain the personification of wit and wisdom. Shakespeare's fools were obviously wise fools. In *Twelfth Night*, Feste is the paid fool and the only one who knows what's going on, the only one who isn't mad or duped, the commentator who can step back from the turmoil and see things and people for who and what they are.

The jester's cap often has three prongs on it now, but it was once just two and they represented the ass's ears. His rod might have an image or sculpture of himself on it – wouldn't it be fun to use that like a ventriloquist's dummy, allowing the dummy to say and do all sorts of things, and yet there remains the lurking suspicion that you are a fool for merely talking to yourself.

Why not attempt the jester's art by devising riddles, puns and punchlines to deliver gospel truths? It might be in the guise of limericks and knock-knock jokes and other familiar joke structures, but puns provide all sorts of possibilities. The basic principle is that truth can only be conveyed. Humour is an extraordinarily good way of conveying it, and if we get it right, all sorts of things can happen. If a jester got up to do the reading in church you can bet everyone would sit up and take notice, and the jester wouldn't be reading it straight. Jesters are light on their feet because they have to think on their feet as well as somersault on them; they have a lightness of touch that catches us unawares and regales us with laughter as well as truth; and they don't hide their light or even Christ's light under bushels.

## Jokes

Do clowns and fools need jokes? What sort of a question is that? A perfectly reasonable one. Jokes are the stuff and stock in trade of comedians. Without jokes they would very largely die out. For clowns and fools comedy's the thing and it is often best expressed in routines and

situations and 'business'. The trouble with spoken, scripted jokes is that there are very few new ones. Bob Hope is said to have had eight writers constantly writing new material for him. Even with that level of provision, some of his material may not have been the most original since most jokes are derivative or generically related.

It may not be the joke that makes them laugh but the way you tell it, with some quirk of facial contortion, a hint that maybe you don't understand why they're laughing. If they laugh, rejoice. Some people don't even know why they do laugh when the word 'cucumber' or 'ferret' is spoken. Don't worry!

Many of our jokes will be unspoken, visual, if only because it's not always possible to share a joke in words that everyone will hear without you shouting at them. So where you're working out a visual routine, rehearse, rehearse and again rehearse is the key. As the hymn puts it, 'Rehearse, again I say, rehearse!'

## Juggling

(The substance of this section is lifted straight from *Fools Rush In* by Roly Bain because *The Catch* which is the jugglers' magazine described it as 'one of the best written explanations of juggling' so I didn't want to try to improve on it!)

Juggling is one of those things that is wonderfully relaxing once you can do it but you tear your hair out in frustration while you're learning it! Juggling is about throwing not catching – if you get the throw right everything else looks after itself; and it's about rhythm, which is why it is relaxing and people are beginning to use it as an aid for contemplation as well as an antidote to stress.

What you don't do is what you probably learnt in a playground and that is to use two balls and keep passing them round so that you only ever throw with one hand. To get to three, start with one ball, or better still a beanbag which won't bounce or roll away. Try and relax, with your feet apart and with some give in your knees, so that you can always move one way or another without difficulty. If you're stiff as a board you'll never do it!

Throw the beanbag from hand to hand, but try and keep your hands just above waist level and pointing outwards about forty five degrees. What you want to try to achieve is for the beanbag to travel in an arc or rainbow with the minimum movement of your hands. The throw is in the wrist, and it needs to be lobbed up so that it passes just above your head and lands in the other hand without that hand having to move. You mustn't try and snatch it in mid air or grab it like a slip fielder in cricket. Just let it land in the middle of your flat hand so that it is ready to be thrown again without adjustment. You should focus on the point at the top of the arc, so that all you ever really see is the beanbag at the peak of its flight. Don't follow the flight of the beanbag from hand to hand because when you've got more beanbags going you won't know where to look!

You have to trust yourself and your body to look after the catching. You're bound to drop the beanbags lots of times, but that doesn't matter. If your throw is so accurate that the beanbag always lands in the flat of the other hand, you don't have to be a good catcher! I'm told that if you wanted to learn juggling in a Russian circus school you would spend three years, six hours a day just with the one ball. That's how important the throw is!

Once you are happy with one beanbag, take a second one. All you have to do is exactly the same throw with both hands, one after the other – don't throw them at the same time. Throw the first one, and as it reaches the peak of its arc throw the second one underneath it. Both are in the air at the same time, briefly. It is important to establish a rhythm, so count it. It's worth saying out loud, 'one, two', as you throw each one, or 'throw, throw, catch, catch'. If you persist in passing the ball rather than throwing it, try saying 'left, right', telling your hands to throw. Hands are quite obedient really once the brain can get the message through! One thing to realise is that you have much more time than you think, so don't panic with the second one and throw it too quickly or throw it away from you. Just relax and concentrate on two good throws.

Once you've mastered two, try the third. Check which hand you normally throw first with, and put two beanbags in that hand, one in front of the other – the one in front, held by the fingers will be the one to throw first. Once again, concentrate on the throwing not the catching, and try to establish the rhythm. To begin with, you just want to try throwing each beanbag once. If you're going to count it, try 'left, right, left', telling your hands to throw. The psychological block will be to let go of the last one because you will be desperate to catch the second beanbag first. Don't! With three beanbags there is always one beanbag in the air and all you have to do is to clear the hand that the beanbag is travelling to by throwing the beanbag that is in that hand to the other hand – most of the time you are actually holding two beanbags with one in each hand. If you find that you're throwing one forward it is probably out of panic, and if you can't cure it by relaxing, just juggle face in front of a wall. As the beanbag continues to hit the wall, the brain will suddenly realise how stupid this is and correct it! If you're getting backache from continually picking up the beanbags you've dropped, practise over a bed or sofa so that you haven't got so far to bend down. There is a great sense of achievement when you manage three for the first time. The next step is to try to keep going, counting the rhythm, 'one, two, one, two', and continually clearing the hand that the beanbag is travelling to.

Juggling is quite obsessive because of the counting factor – you move from being able to do four throws to six to ten to twenty seven or whatever. We are able to record our progress and achievement. Once you can do it easily there are all sorts of tricks and different ways of throwing, but you can try other books for that!

## Kingship

Why kingship? Because we couldn't think of any other K's? No, because kings and clowns go together, and a good jester is interchangeable with the king.

Kingship is to do with authority, with who is in charge, and when the jester is around no-one is quite sure. The clown is a sure gauge of authenticity, especially of emotion and words and character and intention, and thus a good test of authority – authentic people have no problem with authority.

Try some king games, like the old children's game of 'I'm the king of the castle – and you're the dirty rascal'. Or musical chairs, and see who is finally left sitting on the throne – and wonder how he/she got there. Reverse musical chairs, so that all the people stay in the game but the number of chairs decreases so that in the end everyone has to get on the one seat, even if it means thirty people sitting on one anothers' knees!

Play 'The king's court'. There are two variations. The first allows one person to be the king and the rest his servants and courtiers, and he then has authority to order anyone to do anything he wants – an exercise in absolute power. If it's not done immediately or to the king's satisfaction or the service is not sufficiently humble or it's too servile, or whatever, he can just have the servant killed, with the simple words 'You're dead!' The servants and courtiers have three lives each. The variation on the game is that the servants and courtiers are not given orders but instead have to think up things that would please the King and allow them into the safety and sanctuary of the court. Again each has three lives and the art is to work out what would please not any king but this king – and to be authentic, which doesn't necessarily mean sincere. If you're nervous or frustrated or amused or whatever, utilise what you're feeling and authenticity results, for which the king may well be grateful. The king has enough sycophants already.

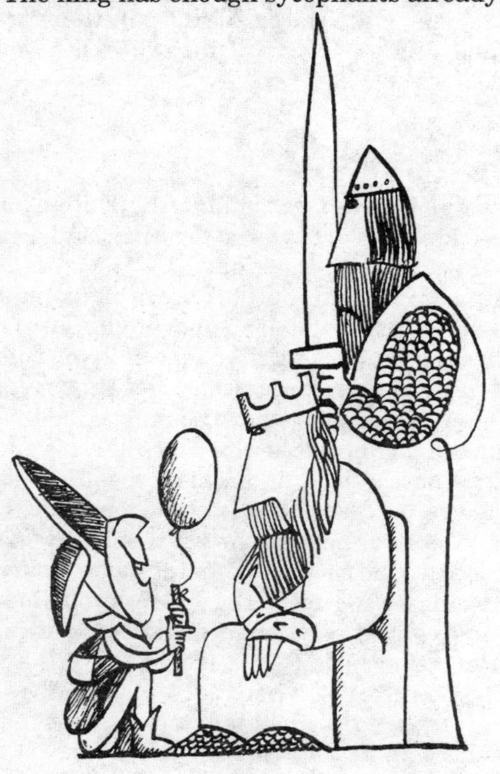

Make traditional crowns with pointed prongs and decide what each prong might stand for, e.g. power, wealth, authority, and thus devise a model of kingship. But then the fool turns the crown upside down and a crown of thorns results, with each of those prongs driving themselves into the victim's head. So what is the model of Jesus's kingship – the opposite, the reverse, the upside-down of what kingship is presumed to be.

What kind of crown or headgear would that demand? Not a crown of thorns by choice. Or, if those prongs of the crown are made nice and tall, then bring on the jester with a pair of shears or scissors to cut the king down to size by chopping off all those prongs apart from one on each side, thus leaving him with the jester's cap and bells to show him what a fool he is.

## K.I.S.S.

The gospel message is in some respects extremely simple. As an exercise, see how few words express what the gospel is for you. It might be: God loves me, I love God, I love others, even that extraordinarily difficult lady whose breath smells of garlic, who wears carpet slippers to church in the snow and who sings the Magnificat out of tune. Come on! I said see how few words!

Too often clowns and fools set out with a simple idea and then complicate it to the point where the simple message is lost in the execution. Hence the slogan K.I.S.S., or 'Keep It Simple, Stupid'. It's a good slogan to remember, a safe principle to apply, and, amazingly easy to remember. There's a lesson there somewhere . . .

## Knees

Knees aren't just for praying on, they're for sitting on too! Get everyone into a tight-fitting circle, all facing the same way sideways, so that on the count of three everybody sits down and finds themselves sitting on the knee of the person behind them. If everybody does it together, it works and provides an analogy for Paul's theology of the body – all different parts of different shapes and sizes, yet all bound together, needing each other, working in unison, and miraculously it works. With any luck it doesn't work at least once, but then once it has worked, tell everyone to raise their right arm . . . and then their left leg . . . and no prizes for guessing what happens next!

As a practice run, you could put everyone in a line in order of height with the tallest at the back, who has a chair behind him, and on the signal everybody sits. The circle's more fun, though! It's fun and it's physical and it breaks down barriers.

## Knock-knock

Knock-knock jokes are generally terribly corny and have schoolboy connotations – they're not very subtle, in other words. But a groan's as good as a laugh if the punchline's memorable and the pun atrocious. If you're forced to try an awful accent to make it work, so much the better! Try making up some biblical ones, either with a biblical character as the name at the door or with a biblical quote as the punchline, or both!

Knock, knock.
*Who's there?*
Nathan.
*Nathan who?*
Nathan will separate us from the love of God.

Knock, knock.
*Who's there?*
Bessie.
*Bessie who?*
Bessie are the pure in heart for they shall see God.

And if you think it's all too corny, reassure yourself that those who have ears will hear!

## Laughter

Where does it come from, what is it, why does it matter? Laughter is a precious gift. It's health-giving (read *Anatomy of an Illness* by Norman Cousins, Bantam Books, if you don't believe me). Laughter, my own and other people's, has saved me down the ages. I think I would have topped myself years and years ago if I hadn't been cheered up as a teenager by the Goon Show. Today it's the cartoonist Larsen and Radio 4's 'I'm sorry I haven't a clue' which keep me laughing. That and the everyday nonsense of the church and the world. I miss Les Dawson, Tommy Cooper and Eric Morecambe, all great laughter-makers.

If you can make people laugh by being yourself as a fool or a clown character, or just you, rejoice and be glad for God has given you a very special gift, the ability to help people look at themselves and the world from a new and different perspective, a chance to get things into proportion, to take themselves less seriously.

Laughter is miraculous. It can well up inside me for no apparent reason, pure joy. I used to take assemblies once a week in the local village school, and no matter how down I felt whenever I went in, the children always lifted me up, helped me to laugh, helped me not to be weighed down by the nonsenses all around. So laughter is a gift from God, and indeed and often from others to us. Laughter is a great defuser of tensions. 'You've got to larf, otherwise you'd go mad!' I've heard that so many times, and it's true. It doesn't magic away awfulness but it puts awfulness into its proper place, where ultimately it can't win. And if you can help all this to happen, blessed are you!

## Letting go

'Letting go' could mean letting go of balloons in people's faces, but that might not be much fun unless it's done playfully and the victim enjoys it. Or it could mean letting people go, which you have to if they don't want to play – you can only invite people to come, you have to let them go.

Letting go is to do with yourself, not somebody or something else, though the effect is the same as the balloon raspberrying its way through the air or the person going the way he chooses. If you choose to let go of yourself, perhaps that carefully crafted and created self that you've managed to survive with so far, then foolishness really begins. Much like the leap of faith, we launch into the unknown, prepared to live by our wits and respond to the moment. To let go and wave goodbye to comfort substitutes and safety nets and dull custom is to experience the liberation of laughter and the exhilaration of folly. But no-one loves a kamikaze clown – to stay on a tightrope you have to focus on the end of the journey, there is an end in sight, and we have to know where we're going even if we don't quite know how we're going to get there. Nobody wants to see you fall for they're with you all the way, and when you reach the other end, there's rapturous applause – and then you let go once more and set off again, and again, and again. The clown is forever leaping over precipices, only to discover there's another and another and another – and he'd be disappointed if there wasn't.

To be a clown is to let go and launch yourself into the vulnerable places, and it's there that you find it's simply the best place to be, the only place to be, and you wonder why you hung on for so long! The world is a place to cling to and its ways cling on to you, and it's much more sensible to stay on the ground; but the heavens are a place to reach for – with both hands. But only a fool lets go . . .

## Licence

It's great fun being a clown, but it is also an enormous privilege. Part of the beauty but also the risk of clowning is that the clown is given licence, sometimes absolute licence, to do whatever he or she wants. It is a licence that has been hard-earned by clowns through the ages, and should never be abused.

The jester's licence was that he could speak the truth to the king and he'd get away with it, if the truth was told with humour and the king got the joke. The clown has access to all sorts of privileged places – homes, churches, cathedrals, prisons, hospitals, wherever it may be, and the clown has to keep getting it right or he gets his head chopped off and it may be no other clowns will ever be allowed to follow where he has been. That doesn't mean he plays safe because the clown must often risk offence for instance, in order to speak the truth or to push people over the edge beyond their blinkered horizons, but it does demand sensitivity and, ultimately, experience. The clown's licence isn't a nice piece of paper like a driving licence that we can flash at the police to show that we're legal and have passed the test, and then motor on regardless. It's what the clown depends on and lives by – a clown without licence is a clown in a straitjacket, and that's no use to anyone when the key's been thrown away.

The clown's licence gives him the key to all kinds of secret places and people, and sometimes he finds he even has the keys to the kingdom. The clown may not be orthodox but in all sorts of foolish ways he is the nonconformist who has the licence to go where angels fear to tread, to turn everything on its head, and to speak of the truth that seems so clear to him. As long as the clowning has integrity and is basically truthful, that licence will never be taken away.

## Limericks

Limericks are silly little five line verses that provide an ideal structure and framework to deliver a worthy and surprising punchline in the last line, and as such are worthy vehicles for biblical humour. Reduce a Bible story to its essence, maybe allowing for the fool's licence, and see what happens. Ideally limericks are laughtermakers and make perfect icebreakers – 'Let's start with a verse from scripture' is the solemn announcement, and then deliver the limerick with all the aplomb or lunacy at your disposal! They work if they are true to the original and if the punchline is appropriate to the story – punchlines should be punched, don't waste them. My favourite limerick is:

Zaccheus, of diminutive stature,
Was reduced to a state of high rapture;
He climbed up a tree,
Took our Lord home for tea,
And gave more taxes back than old Thatcher!

Another one might be:

A millionaire miser called Fred
Stashed all of his cash in the shed.
But when came the day
for which he'd saved all his pay,
They found poor old Fred dead in bed.

My only clue to you is that once you've got the first line make sure you can think of two other rhymes that go with it, especially the punchline rhyme. So if you start off with 'There was an old seaman called Noah', was he a bit of a goer and a terrible rower? It's a chance to brainstorm and have fun and discover some of the humorous possibilities of the Bible in the process. For the clown nothing and everything is sacred, and that includes the Bible, as long as the truth is told, with humour and integrity.

## Lonely

In any audience, any congregation, there will be a shy or lonely person, someone who, for whatever reason, finds it hard if not impossible to join in, to feel part of whatever is going on, someone who feels outside of the 'in' crowd. The sensitive clown or fool will not bludgeon this person into a false membership of the group. He or she will gently seek to draw them in, invite them in without pressure or embarrassment.

It may be that they have never felt able to join in on the group's terms, or may have been damaged by some over-jolly and false feeling of fellowship in the past, discovering that such fellowship was shallow or brittle, unable to meet his or her needs, while promising much and delivering little.

Clowning and fooling is always a gentle invitation to play, to join the dance without pressure, without strings. Sensitive fooling and clowning make the graceful point that there is no one group or individual that has all the answers. Were that the case, this world would not be in the mess it so clearly inhabits today.

Clowns and fools must always respect other people's space, understand their inhibitions and the possible damage that underlies shyness and reticence. We never seek to embarrass those whose journey may seem stalled as we gallop past. The kingdom of God belongs to the poor in spirit while the gentle and meek shall inherit the earth.

The tramp in his loneliness and the bag lady in her desperation stand for a large number of people, and clowns can and should represent them too.

## Love

'All you need is love,' sang the Beatles and I believe they were right. Whatever we do, do it with love. St Augustine once said,'Love God and do what you like' and there's much to be said for that approach to life, provided the saying is understood in the way it was intended. Everything we do, whether in church or outside, whether in work or at play must somehow be shot through with love of God and neighbour and self, no mean task, no mean calling. But possible, I pray.

When love threads through everything we do, audiences, congregations are there as gifts for us to cherish rather than to manipulate or grumble about. One of the hardest sayings of Dietrich Bonhoeffer was, roughly translated, 'God doesn't give you congregations to complain about'. Conversely, and this may be harder still, God doesn't send us priests to criticise.

God knows what it is to be the vulnerable lover. God knows the pain of unrequited love. Whole sections of the Old Testament echo with his longing for his people who are so easily diverted into whoring after the Canaanite gods. What can it be like to be God set about with such a chosen people? And before we rise to condemn, when did I last thank God for all his mercy and loving kindness to me? Jesus watching the crowds move on to the next travelling attraction, letting the rich young man go his own way, looking out across the waste of Golgotha, knew about vulnerable loving. That love in all its vulnerability is something for clowns and fools to discover, taste and handle.

Clowns and fools are called to love those to whom we are sent, whatever they may think of us. We are to live the gospel message however we understand it and trust God and love the audience and let them go. We cannot make them love God, believe the gospel, laugh at our antics and our jokes. We offer what we have and they are free to take it or reject it. Either way, God gives us them and the moment to love. And that is enough.

## Madness

Hands up who's mad! Thank you. Now hands up who's normal! Thank you. Just testing. The results will be taken down, analysed and fed into the reader profile by the publisher. Hang about! That's mad, surely? How can the publisher know what we've just been doing, and anyway won't this book be read by one person at a time? So how can anyone know if I've just put my hand up, and what question I was answering? It's mad, this book, isn't it?

Cosy definitions and assumptions of what is mad and what is normal no longer look safe. What's sensible about the way big business pollutes the planet in the race for profits? What's sane about the way basic necessities are priced beyond the reach of more and more people? Does it really make sense to have so many people engaged in making weapons of ever greater sophistication while the language of death is sanitised, cleaned up so as not to offend anyone?

Why are Christians still divided from each other? Why do we spend so much effort and energy in maintaining differences when we should be celebrating our rich complementary diversity together?

Clowns and fools are well placed to look into the abyss of madness. We aren't, mustn't be bothered about our own status, we move around the bottom of the Christian heap. We don't fit into the hierarchy of church dignitaries. It's our responsibility to spot the madness that masquerades as sense, the nonsense that seems to be normal.

Our calling is to celebrate the divine madness of a God who loves us so much he would see his Son die for us, a God who detests solemn assemblies, loves parties, hates sin, loves the sinner. Our calling is to identify the human madness that keeps us isolated from one another and from God, and to move heaven and earth to leap barriers, invite people in to share our joy and the tears that true love invariably brings.

## Magic

People have all sorts of expectations of clowns and one of those is that they can do magic. And that's fine, as far as it goes. The problem with Christian clowning is that you run up against the obstacle that it confuses or at least blurs the distinction between magic and mystery. One is man-made, the other isn't – or shouldn't be!

If clowns are doing magic, it should be quite clear that it is all an illusion, a trick, a con, and it shouldn't be mistaken for the truth or, more importantly, the Truth with that capital T. The conjuror who happily does the old trick of apparently turning water into wine reduces the original miracle to a parlour game. Did you know that the traditional magic words 'hocus pocus' derive from 'hoc est corpus', which is the Latin for 'This is my Body'? You have to ask yourself the question whether Holy Communion is actually just a bit of magic, a con, or whether it really is part of the Holy Mysteries – mystery or magic? The answer is vital to a living real faith.

Magic that is done by clowns must be comedy or spoof magic. Magicians are terribly clever – we all know that. And if you're a whiteface clown, that's fine – you can be a clever magician. But if you're an auguste, then you can attempt the tricks, even get them right, but in the process or in the aftermath, the trick must somehow be revealed as a trick (even if not how it was actually done, to please the Magic

Circle!). The patter can include as much comedy as you like, as long as it's appropriate, but the punchline and the confession are vital.

Spoof magic might include improbable routines like presenting the impossible trick in church of choosing the right book at the right time, and then, even more impossible, of finding the right page at the first attempt. Things that are done in the grand magician's style immediately become parody and can begin to say all sorts of things about all sorts of people.

It's laughter and truth that we're after – no-one's conning anyone.

## Masks

Masks are fun to make and anyone can make one, out of all sorts of materials. Card and crayons are simplest, but material, papier mâché and junk are all possibilities. Use string to tie it on around the back of the head, or rubber bands to slip over the ears. It's probably easier to have the faces cut out beforehand, using templates, especially if you can offer a variety of shapes.

Clown masks are simple, and people can be encouraged to do a happy face and a sad face, perhaps reversible. It's a good opening activity for a childrens' workshop because people can take their own time and yet can also knock one up pretty quickly. Encourage people to give their clown a name too. Each mask, like every clown, will be quite different, and they testify to the uniqueness of every individual. One activity that can work quite powerfully is to make happy clown masks and mount them on a cross made of thin garden canes, so they can be carried like ball masks – use sticky tape to stick them on. Then come the appointed time, explain that the happy face represents joy but it is only possible because of the empty cross that is behind it – you can't have the cross without resurrection, and vice-versa. Then each child carries their cross home.

Masks themselves are a powerful medium and you have to be careful with them. They have an almost possessive quality about them and people can be quite taken over. Maskwork needs great clarity of movement and focus but it is immensely rewarding in its creation of character. The clown's greasepainted face is a basic mask and it allows the clown character to take on a life of its own, freeing him to step out into the world from behind the mask that hides and yet identifies him.

## Michaelmas madness

I can't remember when I heard anything much about angels in church other than in Christmas carols. Our ideas about angels are largely conditioned by religious art, paintings, stained glass. We are so used to angels as being winged creatures we forget that the word is from the Greek word for a messenger.

Clowns and fools as God's messengers? Why not? A ragged clown enters the church desperate to say something . . . except he can't quite remember what it is and to whom he has to say it. All he knows is that he or she has a message of great importance from someone who's big and mighty and glorious and wonderful and . . . and . . . and . . . The suspense can be heightened by him asking the other fools and clowns if they want to hear what he has to say from whoever it is he's trying to describe (with words petering out for how can you describe God?) The others are all too busy arguing about the price of altar candles, the revision of the ASB, a working party on churchyard regulations.

Finally, in desperation, the messenger finds an unlikely listener . . . the youngest, the oldest . . . maybe even the clergyperson. He spills out the simplest of messages. 'The sender is great, wonderful, marvellous, who made the world and all the creatures in the universe from the giraffe to the dromedary (as endless a list as the occasion will stand) . . . well, he loves you. And being an angel is open to each of us, friends, godparents, soulmates.'

The message of the angels, simple but worldshaking, brief but life-changing, and it's for everyone. Maybe the messages can be printed on little scrolls and given out to everyone there to take home to look at and remind themselves especially when they are feeling unloved, down and out, dead miserable. God loves me and you. Wheeeeee!

## Ministry

Ministry is a buzz word. Can it be applied to holy clowning and foolishness? Yes. For clowning and fooling for the gospel is about proclaiming in a gentle and often fresh way the love of God for each of us, for creation. We speak of acceptance, repentance, forgiveness, constancy, adventure, pilgrimage. We use laughter and humour, and storytelling, mime, dance, whatever tools and gifts God gives us.

The danger is always to exaggerate the importance of what we do. And at that point of temptation, cue St Paul with his marvellous list of paradoxes appropriate to any ministry . . . the poor who make many rich, having nothing yet owning everything, in pain yet always joyful, scourged but not executed, taken for impostors yet genuine, unknown yet known by all, dying and behold we live (2 Corinthians chapter 6, hurrah for Paul!).

We have no badge of office save perhaps the processional broom which doubles as something with which to clean out the church. No glorious mitre, perhaps a cap and bells, no golden chalice, just a bucket or dustpan. We have a ministry . . . no question, but it is no inalienable right, it's a gift, a calling . . . a way of being fools and clowns and jugglers and storytellers and fire-eaters and mime artists for God, for Christ and his gospel in the power of the Spirit.

## Mirrors

Mirrors are important to us and they're not just aids to vanity – they can provide healthy doses of reality! And you can't put on your greasepaint without one. Incidentally a cheap way of getting lots of mirrors for a large group is to buy a pack of mirror tiles.

Mirroring is a good workshop exercise. Two people stand opposite each other, and one becomes the full-length mirror reflecting the other. The person looking into the mirror shouldn't try to catch the mirror out with frenzied, sudden or unconnected movements, for the aim is for both to move as one. The mirror shouldn't guess what's going to happen next and pre-empt the movements either. The secret is to maintain eye contact so that the quality of the movement is maintained rather than getting lost in minor details, and to go with the flow of the movement. If you go with the flow of the movement you may well be surprised at what you find you are doing because for once you are giving your body licence to do what it naturally does. Just as in circus skills, the more you let your brain and reason get in the way, the harder it is. One discovery that can be made is whether you are a natural leader who would rather be the one looking into the mirror, or a natural follower who prefers to follow a lead. But the aim is that anyone looking on shouldn't be able to tell who is leading and who is following. It's quite revealing to not just see but to feel how other people move, but then also to become Everyman, to have the capacity to become anyone you want.

A possible conclusion to the exercise is to try the traditional clown routine, where a clown looks into what appears to be a mirror but in fact is broken, and there is another clown reflecting him instead. A sequence can easily be worked out with a few apparent slips by the mirror which are enough to get the clown thinking, and there needs to be a denouement to finish, such as sticking your tongue out, a squirt of water or whatever. There needs to be enough synchronised movement in the first place to establish the hoax and the game, but then all sorts of things are possible.

The clown himself is a mirror who, if he's getting it right, holds up that mirror to his audience so that they can see themselves in him, and as they laugh at the clown they begin to laugh at themselves in recognition of their own foolishness and predicament. A standard clown routine is based on a clown looking in a mirror and laughing gleefully before proclaiming 'Here's a picture of the greatest fool in the world'. Then the clown happily shows it round his audience so that they can see themselves.

## Names

Names are precious. They define you and personify you. Your own name was given to you at birth by people who love you and brought you into being. To be known by your name establishes a relationship of some kind, and there are a number of myths and children's stories which revolve around the power of knowing and calling someone by their name, whether it's the fairy story of Rumpelstiltskin or the stories of Susan Cooper and Ursula le Guin.

When you become a clown you have a chance to choose a name for yourself. People sometimes choose a name that is akin to their own, so a Christopher might decide to be Christo. Others use another of their given names that they are never called by, or make a pun of their surname. You could choose something totally different or absurd, like Sausage or Mr Micklechip or Rednosewrangler. But whatever you choose, allow it to occur to you, and let your instinct be the arbiter of whether it's the right name for your clown character or not. Don't call yourself Sunshine if you're a sad old tramp clown, unless there's an unmistakeable gleam in your eye! And keep it simple. You can, of course, use your own name too – if you and others can cope with it. You soon get to know if you've plumped for the wrong name if it just doesn't feel right and people react strangely. If it's wrong, change it, until you get it right.

There are a a number of name games that are good icebreakers. One with beanbags becomes a kind of communal juggle. You start with one beanbag and people have to say their own name before throwing it to someone else – it's a simple introduction. Once everyone's had a chance to learn everyone else's name, the rules change so that you have to say the name of the person you're throwing the beanbag to – if you can't remember, you're encouraged to ask. Where it goes mad is that then another beanbag is introduced and then another and another – indeed as many as you like – and absolute bedlam ensues. The secret is to catch the eye of the person you're throwing to as you call, before you throw. It certainly breaks down the barriers and forces people to know the others by name!

It's so easy to give away your name, and yet some people find it so difficult. You'd have thought that Christians at least would like to be known by their Christian name rather than by their title, but in so many places they don't.

What happens when the clown steps in and gives them all names that suit them? There's no reason why she can't, if she loves them.

## Never mind jollity . . . be joyful

Hands up who hasn't met a clown or a Christian who gives the impression that he has a large aerosol can in his bag labelled 'Jollyspray'. There's something hugely troubling about jolliness which you suspect to be false, painted, sprayed on like so much make-up. I'm no expert on face painting but if the joy isn't there inside, deep inside you, no amount of jollyspray or false jollity will fool the people you're working with. Okay, you can put your hands down . . . I should have said so before. Sorry.

And another thing, don't keep apologising when things go wrong in performance. The best mistakes, unrehearsed, often add something, like when I kept being rung up by the media while trying to give a talk about the anatomy of a clown. It was my bad luck to be duty press officer that weekend. Far from being a disaster, these calls added to the joyful atmosphere of the day.

Now in ranting against false jollity, I do understand the down side of being a fool or a clown, those days when I feel I haven't anything to give. And strangely when I'm literally at my wit's end, I usually find I'm rescued, lifted up by those around, fellow fools or clowns or the audience or congregation. I think it's the grace of God at work, and also something to do with there being more chance of honesty when defences are down. And that's about vulnerability and that comes later.

## New eyes for old

I remember visiting an eighty-something-year-old lady in hospital. She had had cataracts removed from both her eyes. In a darkened room she had her bandages removed. 'Can you see anything?' Even if she had said nothing her face would have given the game away: she could begin to see things, people, faces, more clearly.

Clowns and fools can see very clearly. They learn again to see as children see, fresh as for the first time. Try it. Spend time with a flower, get to know an orange. I once asked a group of GPs to get to know an orange, their orange, before passing their orange round the group. The biggest panic was the fear of not recognising their orange when it was passed round the circle back to them. An interestingly perilous game.

Clowns see everything new and fresh for the first time and they can help others to do the same.When did you last really look at a painting, a sunset, a tree and wonder childlike at it, at them? If you answer, 'I'm too busy . . . I haven't time,' that won't do. Make time, take time. Clowns and fools can hold out for a different kind of clock, one that moves at half speed, or maybe moves backwards to a time when wonder was encouraged, was part of life. In church, people can be reminded of the gift of wonder, of curiosity, of excitement at really looking and seeing something, someone, fresh and new. God's gift. Hand out flowers and suggest each one is looked at from every side, from new angles, as if it was the first flower anyone had ever seen. Then give time and space for people to make whatever sense they can out of the experience.

## Next to Godliness?

Fooling and clowning can bring you into very close contact with others. If you want people to laugh and not shrink away from you in horror or disgust, don't chew garlic before a performance. Bad breath is a killer. Personal cleanliness is a must and clothes, however tramp-like need to be clean and smell-free. Given that clowning can be energetic, talcum powder used in advance can prevent fools from being purveyors of pongs! I've often wondered why the Lone Ranger was so called. Was it because he never took a bath, never washed his teeth and always chewed garlic the better to frighten off the evil-doers? If we want to communicate a message, we have to be sure that we radiate joy and love rather than stale sweat and old socks!

## Noses

There is no doubt that most peoples' image of a clown includes a red nose, or at least an artificial nose of some kind. There is something about a nose that is both characteristic and absurd! If you're in search of your clown face, you have to decide what to do with that thing in the middle of your face. Do you want it to be small, so that something else features? Or do you want it large? Or moustached? Or long? Or pointed?

There are lots of noses on the market. The standard red nose is extremely popular and you can get foam ones that just sit on your nose – there's a split in the back that goes around it. They look good but are prone to falling off. There are plastic noses that can be tied on with elastic or fishwire or whatever, and that means they are safe as long as you don't mind or can disguise the string going across your cheeks. There are rubber noses too, which come in all shapes and sizes, and some clowns use double-sided tape, even carpet tape, to keep the nose on while others use spirit gum or some other glue to do the trick. If you're quite a physical clown, then the sweat can make them fall off. If you're feeling really ambitious you can make your own nose that's a perfect fit with latex, but that's another story.

Noses are important. They are a basic mask and they are fun to play with and experiment with, finding moods and voices and characters that go with them. But you don't have to have an artificial nose, you can just paint it red, or leave it completely. The trouble with artificial noses is that they are targets for some small and not so small children who delight in making a fool of the clown by pulling his nose off or because they really do want to see if it's real or not. Both wigs and noses are vulnerable and obvious objects of desire, in all sorts of ways! The less removeable and artificial your nose looks, the less likely it is going to be snatched.

## Objects, use of

Some clowns seem to have the power of transforming everything they touch and they manage to persuade us that things are not quite what they seem. It's fun to play with objects and give them a range of different uses so they become quite different things – a tennis racket becomes a guitar, which becomes a mirror, which becomes a lollipop, which becomes a machine gun, etc.

As a workshop exercise, pass an object round a circle and each person in turn changes the object into something new – you receive the tennis racket as machine gun and then suddenly turn it into whatever occurs to you. You get rid of the easy and obvious ones first, but then don't give up because that is when the imagination starts to work and the creative juices flow. If someone really gets stuck pass it on. A variation on the game is to put six objects in the middle and people in turn leap into the middle, grab one and use it – but then make the rule that you have to use two objects together.

Another game is 'Usurping the throne'. One person sits on a chair with six objects in front of him and the others have to utilise one or more of the objects in an attempt to make him leave the throne. Anything usually works – a ball becomes a bomb or a surprise pregnancy or you might just shoot for goal and he has to dive to save it. If you succeed, it's your turn to take the throne, until you are scared, lured or chased away.

Once you've had a good go at 'Use of objects', get people to choose one object each, and then go away and make up a story, giving their object five or six different uses to illustrate the tale. It's best to decide on the different uses first and then build a story around it. Once you've done that, try doing a biblical story in the same fashion. The key to performing with transforming objects is conviction. As long as you believe that that large red wig is Moses in a basket in the bulrushes, then we can; but if you have any doubt about it, then so will we. Only a fool would believe it, but that's what makes it work. It's like a child's game, where everything is absolutely real to the child because she can see it clearly. The clown needs that simple wonder and imagination to see it clearly so that we can see it clearly too.

## Offence

Yes, people took offence at Jesus and what he said and did. But while people may be offended at what we say and do, it must never be the aim of the clown or fool to cause offence, not unless we want to feel that millstone around our necks. As clowns and fools we are guests in schools, hospitals, prisons, churches. As such, we must behave with sensitivity and grace, not crash around wrecking people's grasp on faith, assaulting their dearly held beliefs with crass or loud humour. We are there to gently question, perhaps widen a horizon, encourage people to look again at something which has become truly stale but which has the power to revive, refresh and resurrect.

And this means hard work in discovering as much as we can about the people to whom we go, discovering where they are on their pilgrimage, what they expect from us, what would help, restore, build up, encourage. To do any less is unworthy.

## Opera

Lots of people like to sing in the bath or croon along to their car radios, but people get very embarrassed about singing in public unless they've had far too much to drink and there's a karaoke machine within singing distance. The trouble with singing in church is that people think they have to sing in tune, and if there aren't enough people to cover our feeble attempts at melody, we leave it to others – and then nobody sings! We're worried about making fools of ourselves, and yet singing is a wonderful uplifting gift and music can move us to places beyond our imagining.

Utilising this fear of making fools of ourselves, get would-be clowns to create a spontaneous opera! Give yourselves a bit of greasepaint or a hat or a nose or some bit of basic costume to help you get into the mood, and then gather in a circle. Each person in turn then attempts a blast of grand opera – it's got to be in the grand style with plenty of oomph because it's the exaggeration that helps the exercise. You just have to go for it! Once warmed up a little, try an operatic conversation between two people – it needn't be in words, though words help a storyline. Finally build it up so that everyone joins in and a whole tortuous, probably melodramatic plot, ensues. Characters are allowed to step in and out of the action – they will probably be desperate to step out! – or the 'stage' gets too cluttered. It's a good exercise too for deciding who has the focus of attention at any given moment, for the performers can't all sing at once and drown each other out. Those who like to upstage others are soon found out and should be dealt with immediately! It's also an exercise where you have to respond to and obey your instincts when you know exactly what needs to happen next and then you have to step in – if you hesitate, the moment is past and it's too late. It's a case of the clown leaping into the circus ring, the vulnerable place, regardless of whether it's strictly his turn or whatever, because he knows he is needed immediately. He may not know how or why or what, but he knows the when and it's now!

If you're feeling really brave, why not take a biblical story as the main plot and storyline, but allow various absurd subplots to develop? You could end up with a glorious operatic parable to perform in church which can become rehearsed and choreographed, while still allowing for spontaneity within that framework.

## Pies

People always associate clowns with custard pies, but this isn't under 'C' for custard because custard is sticky and messy and expensive and ugh! Shaving foam is easier and cheaper and it brushes off clothes when it's dry, but use regular shaving foam – it usually says 'regular' on the canister. If you use mentholated or perfumed foam it stings the eyes and is horrid. The more traditional mixture is Lux flakes with a bit of glycerine to give it shape and substance.

Shaving foam on paper plates are the easiest pies – use tinfoil plates and they're washable and reusable! Allow the shaving foam canister to reach or remain at least at room temperature – the warmer it is, the better it works and the longer it lasts. Don't buy the cheapest because it may well be no good! If you want to make it look big without using all the contents of the canister, start a spiral with foam from the outside going in, so that you leave a hollow middle but the foam is all heaped up. You can shape it, smoothe it and mould it, even dab your finger in it to make it come up in peaks like meringue. If you want a really huge-looking pie, use a circle of sponge as the base (the kind you wash with, not the the kind you bake cakes with!) and then just cover it with a thinnish layer of foam. It still does the trick.

The golden rule on delivering pies is 'splat not slam'. It's no fun being the victim or the audience if you end up with a bloody or broken nose. The point of a pie is for laughs – essentially it's a parody of violence, so to be violent with a pie is to miss the point entirely. So don't slam the pie, whacking it into somebody's face, splat it instead. When you splat, it's more of a placing or pushing so the pie hits the face but the plate stops short, allowing the foam to spread over the face. If you then twist the pie a little bit, still being careful not to twist the face underneath, you leave more of the foam on the face as you take the plate off. It helps to have large hands to grip the plate because you need to hold the plate with the flat of your hand – don't hold the plate by the edge or you end up with a fist and a punch.

If you're delivering the pie, make some sort of physical contact first, e.g. put your free hand on the victim's shoulder just before you deliver it, both to give a warning that it's coming but also to help you judge the distance and get your range. If you're receiving the pie, try not to telegraph the fact that you know it's coming, because it's meant to be a surprise. And make sure that your mouth is closed – if you inhale it, it really is very nasty and you can't breathe, your chest just burns. All the more reason to warn the victim first, especially if you're coming from behind him, and to do it properly rather than just mess around. Pranks with pies can be very unpleasant and dangerous.

Pies don't have to be delivered in the middle of your face, of course. They are there to be sat on, trodden in, and so on. They can be splatted on the side of your face too: cue, 'turn the other cheek'.

If it's a hot summer's day and you want to practise outside, make a dustbin full of soap and have lots of messy fun. In a twenty gallon bin, grate three bars of shaving soap into about three inches of water. Let it soak and get a bit mushy. Then mix with a handmixer or, better still, a drill with a paintmixer attachment, and whirr it round so it gets lots of air inside it. It takes a while, but it should foam up enough to all but fill the bin. I'm told that food colouring doesn't stain clothes, so you could add a little bit to make it more dramatic. Then line up the participants in two rows facing each other and dish out paper plates. Have a dry run first, without the foam, to give people a chance to see if they can hold the plate and how they're going to do it – basic choreography. Then let everyone get a plateful of foam, and each gives and receives one. Then let anarchy reign. Opinions may vary, but it's a way of demonstrating that it's better to give than to receive!

## Piety: good and bad

There's a dreadful disease that sometimes afflicts people as soon as they enter church or become responsible for any church activity. They cease to be the friendly person that you once knew and begin to act in a strange manner, a censorious, disapproving person singularly lacking a sense of humour. It happens to us clergy sometimes. When we climb into a pulpit or don our strange ecclesiastical costume, our voices tighten up and become clerical and our ability to laugh is somehow stifled.

I can only think this is a nasty attack of false piety, some kind of holy split personality, a vestry Jekyll and Hyde syndrome. Life is one, personality is one. I am the same silly person whatever I'm wearing, wherever I am. I don't put piety on with my cassock, any more than I put on laughter with a clown suit.

Piety, true holiness is probably a gift, not something to be striven for and if there's one thing Jesus couldn't and maybe cannot stand it's self-righteousness, holier than thou, look at me praying, giving to charity more than that wastrel over there.

False piety is a legitimate target for laughter, for unseating because it divides us from each other and from God. Whatever else we are about as clowns and fools it mustn't be that. If you feel an attack of false piety coming on, get ready to duck. A custard pie will be along shortly.

## Plates

Plates are fun to play with. You can manipulate a plate on the flat of your hand all round your body. You can do a forward roll with a plate and still keep the food on it. You can balance a plate on the crook of your arm like a waiter, let it slip and catch it just before it hits the ground. You can throw them to each other like frisbees. And, of course, you can spin them.

Don't use your best china when you want to spin a plate – in fact, don't use your best china for any of the above! When you start spinning plates, get a plastic one that is designed for the purpose and the stick that goes with it. If the stick is a wooden one rather than the bendy plastic sort, the plate goes on the pointed end. Hang the plate on the stick, so that the point is inside the lower rim of the plate. Hold the stick as vertically as you can. Then you have to get the plate moving – which doesn't mean flying across the room! The knack is that it's all done with the wrist. If you point your index finger up the stick, it helps. You just need to trace the inside of the rim of the plate – it's quite a small circle, and the smoother you can make it, the better. As soon as the plate gets to horizontal and starts to almost hover, then stop the stick still and the plate continues to spin. You don't have to move the stick to the middle, it does it for you.

It will be quite frustrating at first. One common mistake is to try and spin it too quickly: it is a kind of whipping motion but to whip it too quickly means it will fly off. You can be quite gentle with it, and it may only need two or three circular turns. Another common problem is that people tend to push the stick up as far as they can reach in the process, and again the plate flies off, but this time upwards. Try to keep your arm stable, so that only the wrist is moving. Another difficulty is that poeple waggle the stick rather nervously from side to side when it should be a circular motion. Or again, people make the circular motion much too big, putting all of their strength into it. You've made real progress when the plate starts to go around the stick, but if you find that the plate never seems to reach the horizontal or, in your terms, the stick never gets to the middle, then it's because you're not using your wrist enough – there's too much arm and elbow, and they can't really move quickly enough. Try and release the wrist, which allows the stick to circulate that much more freely and quickly, and all of a sudden you'll find you've done it!

Once you've got it spinning, throw it up in the air and catch it again. As long as you push the plate up far enough in the air without catching the side of it, and catch somewhere near the middle of the plate with the stick as it lands, it should work. Don't try and spear the plate as it lands, but cushion it a bit as you would a cricket ball. While the plate is up in the air, turn the stick upside down so it lands on the other end. If two of you can do it, throw it to each other, and if you throw it high enough it looks good and makes it easier. You could add all sorts of acrobatic moves to make up a sequence – presentation is at least half the art. As the plate starts to slow down, just whip it up again and carry on – include it as part of the choreography. You can either do that by using the same technique as when you started, or you can do it by pushing the side of the plate with the flats of your fingers. It would make a good offertory as your offering of your gifts, and you could finish by actually taking the collection in the plates. But don't try and spin them when they're full even if you do want to encourage the congregation to throw their money around!

If you want a much more clowning sequence, incorporate some missed catches and spins, throw in a few distractions and diversions, and you're away. You could try a whole routine with a whiteface clown trying to teach an auguste how to do it with all the obvious frustrations and opportunities that would arise. The auguste could give up in the end, happy enough because of all the fun he's had, and then the whiteface would storm off in extreme exasperation. But then the auguste spots an arrangement of flowers, smells them, plucks a lily from the midst and suggests to the congregation, 'Consider the lilies of the field: they don't toil, they don't spin, but Solomon in all his glory was not attired like one of these . . . '

## Play and playfulness

Children learn about the world through playing. And suddenly when school ends, play ends too. It's as if someone has decreed that we know all we're ever going to know and now we must stop playing, grow up and become as boring as all the other adults. What a tragedy!

True there are adult games, individual and team sports which sometimes look for all the world like scaled down world wars, fought to the final defeat and victory. Adults have other games too, games of manipulation, games with dark purposes, like strategies for selling people things they neither need nor really want. There are selling games, management games, power plays.

Clowns and fools are about play which increases trust, excites wonder, stimulates questioning, builds up confidence. Elsewhere in this book you will find some examples. There are libraries of games with wholly gospel innocent purposes, and games which are just thoroughly enjoyable for their own sake.

Part of a foolish and clown attitude to life is that of playfulness which is about becoming as a child, ready to question, quick to wonder and forgive and slow to bear grudges or harbour resentment.

I've often wondered about God and play. Wasn't God playing when he created the universe, the stars and the galaxies, designed the giraffe and the hippopotamus, you and me?

Play and playfulness are ways of drawing out creativity, of setting God-given imagination free to roam where it will. And once this begins to happen, the oppressive rules that govern so much contact and communication are overturned and new things become possible. The questions 'why not?' and 'what if?' become the watchwords for the clown and the fool whether organising a day's work or revolutionising the local church. And why not?

## Prayer

With it, anything is possible. Without it, some things simply won't happen, as in the case of the boy cursed with fits the disciples were unable to heal. When Jesus healed the boy, his friends were puzzled. Jesus' answer suggested that maybe they hadn't prayed. This demon could only be driven out by prayer.

The demons are still with us, pride, selfishness, greed, envy, malice. Clowns and fools are prone to all of these and more, particularly because we are performers, easy prey for fantasies around our own strength, when what we know is weakness, something God can work with, use for his purpose and his glory.

If prayer meant so much to Jesus, how can we his followers neglect it? I have to answer, with the greatest of ease, and with a resulting dis-ease in myself and in what I attempt as fool or clown. Be warned, then. And be comforted and encouraged too, for prayer need not be wordy, or necessarily well structured or coherent. It is precisely in our apparent inability to pray that God's Spirit prays for us, with us, in us.

## Preparation

I have often wondered what it must be like to be a dumb minister of the gospel, a mute preacher of the word of God. I'm fascinated by mimes, their ability to communicate the deepest hopes and fears and emotions without the help or props that are words. One thing is clear. If they are going to communicate in silence, then they must know with every fibre of their being just what it is they want the audience to understand.

When fools and clowns work with words and actions, the need for preparation is perhaps even more vital, because the words that accompany the actions can so easily mislead, distract, confuse, contradict.

We must not let what we do be spoiled by lack of preparation. It's tempting to think that improvisation needs no preparation. In my book, it needs more: more time to think through what might happen, where I want to go, what I want to say, what I want people to understand even if I don't know how it will be said.

God will help us in what we attempt. But I believe God wants some evidence of our commitment to effective clown and fool ministry, in preparation, in prayer, in thinking it through and doing the very best to the point where he can take and make of it what he will to his glory. And if you want a clown's prayer to add to your collection, try this one from Clowns International:

> Dear Lord, I thank you for calling
> me to share with others the most
> precious gift of laughter.
> May I never forget that it is your gift
> and my privilege.
> As your children are rebuked for their self importance
> and cheered in their sadness,
> help me to remember that your foolishness is
> wiser than our wisdom. Amen.

It is used every year at their service on the first Sunday in February at the Clowns' Church, Holy Trinity, Dalston, London. Everyone is welcome!

## Prisons

No jokes about captive audiences, please! If you are invited to perform inside a prison, just as much prayer and preparation will be needed as for any other group. A worthwhile step in preparation is to sit quietly and try to write down exactly what you feel about prisons and prisoners. It may be that with your feelings, you shouldn't venture into a prison.

The fact that they can't easily escape if they don't like what you do doesn't mean you can lower standards. In preparing, try to discover exactly what the chaplain is looking for. Find out as much as you can about the class of prisoners being held. They may very well be being held on remand, innocent until proved guilty. Whatever you do, make time to listen and talk to the prisoners afterwards. This may be more important and rewarding than the performance.

With prison audiences, as with other audiences, it's vital not to think of them as gospel fodder whom you can bash over the head and take stunned into the kingdom. They may very well know more about forgiveness and repentance than you do. They have probably had more time than you'll ever have to think about such things. Be sensitive, be funny and be gentle. And don't be shocked to discover that they've lifted you up rather than the other way round.

## Problem-solving

Give a clown a problem to solve and he'll get there in the end but he's got to get there and do it in his own foolish way according to his own peculiar logic. It's much more fun to go all the way round the houses to visit the person next door because all sorts of things might happen on the way – it's boring to go straight to the gate and in.

Some of the great routines that clowns have done have been based on a simple problem or task and the comedy has arisen from the distractions and blind alleys and cul-de-sacs he's ended up in along the way. There's a perverseness of logic in the clown – it's consistent and rational but it's all upside-down. It only works if we can see the reasoning behind his action, even if we are amazed by it – especially if we are amazed by it! Grock, on discovering that his piano stool wasn't near enough to the piano to allow him to reach the keys, got up, moved to the other side of the piano and started to try and heave it nearer to the stool!

Ask a clown to go up into the pulpit – how is he going to get there? He might try blowing up a balloon, hold it above his head and try to float up – if he tries that there's a lot of fun to be had simply in blowing up the balloon and tying a knot in it. He might try a high jump, a prayer, even a handy ladder, but he'll enjoy the play of the challenge. He'll enlist the help of his audience, even if he turns a deaf ear to the advice being bawled at him by the children who can see it's much easier to go up the pulpit steps! Problems are simply opportunities – a chance for adventure rather than a cause of stress – or at least they can be! If he doesn't solve the problem, it doesn't really matter either to him or to us because it's been such fun along the way. And maybe that puts the original problem into perspective.

## Processions and pomposity

Bishop Robert Hardy of Lincoln included a jester in his enthronement service procession in Lincoln Cathedral in 1987. He said, 'I wanted to have a clown at my enthronement to enable me to greet people in an informal way, and to remind all at the service that amidst the pomp and ceremony all of us (including bishops) have feet of clay and need recalling to our common humanity.' I expect one or two of those present were a little outraged at what happened but the bishop had a point.

Each of us is in one sense or another a servant of the servants of God. Not so much a little lower than the angels but the lowest of the low. We aren't preoccupied with status or position. And when great occasions take place, it's all too easy for a hint of pomposity to creep into the proceedings. I remember a time when some Holy Fools were invited to take

part in the Prison Chaplains' Annual Conference in Nottingham. We spent an afternoon taking part in an otherwise organised market place. We encouraged whoever we met to play a little and enter our foolish world. Later we took part in the conference service which had its formal procession of dignitaries present. The fools thought they should process too behind the main procession led by the cross. I thought it important that we should follow some appropriate symbol. What better than a large mop to symbolise the servant role? So, with mop held high, and bucket carefully carried, the fools entered.

Later that evening some of us prevailed on the canteen staff to let us help with serving at table, and in very short order we learned how to balance five or six main courses on one arm, and served with enormous skill and grace. Quite right too.

There's probably no better antidote to status hunger and pomposity than the picture of the true servant. Fools should not be above footwashing, washing up, mopping up, serving at table, being, as Paul once said, 'Your servants for Christ's sake.'

## Quality control

Whatever we do, let it be the very best. When we clown, when we fool, when we tell stories, fall over, juggle, mime, whatever we do, we do it for God's sake. It must be the very best. Which is why planning, preparation, rehearsal and design all matter. Nothing is worse than a slipshod performance, or arriving late without some very very good reason.

I once went to a Christingle service and arrived so early I was able to improvise my entrance and make it twenty times more effective than if I had simply arrived on time and walked on. Looking around the unfamiliar vestry where I was concealed in order to seem as if I hadn't arrived at all, I found a large broom, a ladder, a door to the outside car park, and in a few minutes I was able to devise an entrance which sounded and looked like I'd had a fight with some villain in the car park on my way to the church and literally backed into the chancel with a very long ladder. The first thing I saw was the altar so I had to stop and bow. Turning around I caught sight of the people . . . frightening lot. So there was a lot of curiosity aroused, a sense of heightened expectancy which helped what followed to work.

Entrances and exits do matter. If you're in a rush through being late, they're likely to be messed up. They need time and thought which must be budgeted for in advance. Three minutes worth of improvisation may well take a day of hard thinking and preparation beforehand.

Casing the joint, knowing whether you can be heard at the back, discovering where the sound system is and how it works, enlisting help with light switches, making sure everyone in the group knows when and where to arrive – these are all vital considerations if we are concerned with excellence. Nothing less will do.

## Questions

Foolishness and fooling are not about certainty or answers, rather more they are about questions. If we communicate by our foolishness then what we do and say, and what we don't do and say will lead to questions. And that's great. If people ask a question, then they are motivated, by curiosity, inquisitiveness or whatever. And that's a strong signal even when the question sounds like it's an impossible question to answer. There's nothing wrong in all the world with not knowing all the answers. Think for a moment about your feelings when you see or hear an 'expert' who appears to know everything, the answer to every question. Many of Jesus' stories or parables led to people, often his disciples, asking him questions. Jewish rabbis are often asked what their stories mean, and rather than give a direct answer, they tell another story. The motive, I'm almost sure, is to let the seeker do the work of discovery. That way, the answers, whatever they are, are likely to mean more than if they had been served ready-made on a plate.

However, one reaction to this approach may be a terrible infantile regression: 'You're the expert, tell me the answer, I can't work it out for myself . . . and I'll be sick all over my frock and your trousers if you don't tell me NOW!' Stay with it, don't give in. Some answers have to be found by the seeker, if he or she is to learn and grow in faith.

Whatever the questions, don't, please, answer with ready-made, pre-digested answers that sound as if you've given them out to a succession of bored ignoramuses . . . or ignorami? Beware the ready answer prompted by a wish to be superior. The clown and the fool illuminate, explore, play with questions and are also looking for some tentative and maybe partial and temporary answers. Clowns and fools have to journey and grow and question too.

## Resurrection

The clown in the circus ring always gets up whatever has happened to him. A plank in the face, a bucket of water over his head, down her trousers, an exploding car or the simple banana skin – nothing keeps the clown down. The clown always rises again to face life and the slings and arrows. The clown is a resurrection figure and the worst tragedy of all is for a clown to die in the circus ring. Please don't do it! Even if you desperately want to stay lying there because it's comfortable, risk free (it never is) or you hurt in every joint, tradition, this book and most of all God, require you to stand up.

Resurrection isn't just what happened on a rubbish tip of a hill two thousand years ago. It's what Christians need to discover for ourselves as a daily event. It may be that we go to a meeting expecting that it's going to be the very worst meeting we've ever been to in our life, and that takes some doing. To our amazement and delight, it is actually one of the best meetings we have known. Colleagues, complete strangers say positive things. There is an amazing determination to progress the business, to listen to every contribution. I go to see someone in the parish expecting to be bawled out for not visiting her since God knows when and she makes me welcome, is delighted to see me, against all the odds. She makes the tea and I feel like a cross between a louse and a king. When I expect to experience death, I find instead a kind of resurrection. If God is to be believed, these little deaths tow their little resurrections in their wake. The trouble is I don't always believe God.

Dying, we live. And our resurrection life is here and now. We need the practice, the rehearsal time now. And the world needs to learn that resurrection is a fact of life. The gospel is about overcoming all the little deaths along the way and clowns and fools share a calling to make resurrection visible, possible for others.

### Risky business

To be foolish, to clown around is to risk all kinds of responses, ranging from the hysterical to the downright hostile ('Ought to know better than to be wasting his time and mine playing around like that – it's disgraceful!'). Rejection, dependence, delight, tears, laughter or a great and deep silence are all likely responses to what we do and who we are and what we say as clowns and fools. How much more so when as holy fools we touch on deep issues of heart and soul? There is a strain of Christianity which is so deeply personal, it appears to be armed against anything which comes close, questions, explores and perhaps threatens. It is not our calling to attack deeply held beliefs. We may question, lovingly and sensitively, but unless we want the millstone-round-the-neck treatment, we don't destroy faith, we don't lead astray. Ours is both a high and lowly calling. We risk, as did the early Christians, being seen as the refuse of the world, earthen pots containing great treasure.

We risk stumbling into very deep pools of feeling and experience. Fooling and clowning can remind people of the child in them, the child who used to laugh and cry and play and feel very lonely and needed comforting and encouraging. That child may have been lost, denied, repressed and a fresh meeting with that child, perhaps in a play session, may give rise to very strong emotions. We all need help in learning to expect the unexpected, to be aware of some of the risks of our work and to be prepared not to be thrown by what happens. And lest you feel faint-hearted, remember that faith without risk is probably the faith of the graveyard.

### Rola-bola

A rola-bola is a board that balances on a cylinder, and then you try to balance on the top. You can make one easily: take a bit of wood (e.g. five-ply timber), three foot long and eight or nine inches wide; screw a batten on each end, a couple of inches from the end – these act as brakes to stop the board slipping off the cylinder altogether; and procure a strong cylinder from somewhere that is wider than the plank you've got. British Gas pipe, with permission, is good for this!

The basic principle of all balancing is that you should stand as tall as you can – think 'up' and you've got a chance of staying up; think 'down' and you'll come crashing down. That's true of unicycles, ropes, globes, rola-bolas or whatever. Step on to the board from the end that's resting on the floor, and position your feet with equal weight upon them about two feet (in distance!) apart. You need some give in your knees, and to stand as solidly as you can – if someone was going to come and push you over, there's a way of setting yourself so that you don't just topple over.

It's very important, to begin with, that you have someone standing in front of you to catch you if you go over. Hang on to the shoulders of your helper as you get the feel of the thing moving. The alternative is to use a rail or banister – anything you can grab in an emergency. If you do fall, don't break the fall with a hand or knee or elbow because it will break those bones. If you're going to fall, allow yourself to go, and allow your length of body to cushion the fall.

Back to the balancing board. Find a point somewhere at eye level that you can focus on. This helps you centre yourself. What you want to try to do then is let your legs and hips do the work of controlling the board while the top half of your body always remains above the actual rola (cylinder). However fast the rola-bola might be moving beneath you, you should eventually be able to drink a cup of tea without spilling it! To begin with, take your weight across from one side to the other and get the feel of the movement and the balance. Wherever your weight goes, the board goes. The secret is to keep your weight in the middle, above the rola. If you shoot your weight across, then you and the board will shoot across too, and that's when accidents happen. If the board starts to twist round, it's because you haven't got equal weight on both sides – if you twist, the board twists. Don't look down to see the rola, keep looking at your focus point and feel the balance. What you're trying to achieve is to stand rock solid in the middle, and a minimum of movement will always bring the board back to the middle. The golden rule is 'Never take a foot off the board'. If you do, you'll disappear in one direction, the board in another, the rola in another, and everyone gets hurt. Have the confidence to relax, think up, and believe that you can do it!

Once you can control it, you can play with it and on it. There are all sorts of tricks. You can mount the board by balancing it like a seesaw and then jumping up on to it – much easier than it sounds. It's the only way to get on a bigger rola! Bigger rolas are easier to use because they move more slowly, but you need to be able to do it before you can get on one. You can crouch or kneel on the board, turn lengthwise along the board, jump and spin round 180 or 360 degrees. You can use blocks at either end and put more boards on top! You can also combine skills because your top half is unaffected and your hands are free, so you can juggle, diabolo, balance or whatever. The possibilities are endless – and fun! Once you can do it, you don't have to think about it, and then you can start to tell stories . . .

## Rules

Everyone has rules, even clowns. Every clown organisation in the world has its rules and a code of conduct, all designed to further the art of clowning as well as maintain the clown's high standards and good reputation. Every individual clown will have their own rules of thumb as to what they can do, and what might work, and how far they can go, etc. And rules are necessary – they provide the framework and structure. But any fool knows that rules are made to be broken! When the clown is around, the rules are suspended and a new and different set of rules apply. Clowns are anarchists in the way they turn things topsy-turvy and force us not just to rewrite the rulebooks but to rethink the way we look at things and the way we live our lives.

So when you're clowning, don't be bound by normal rules and conventions because clowns push back the frontiers and keep resetting the boundaries. You'll know if you've gone too far, or at least you should do with experience. But go for it! The Good News is that faith is not about the letter of the law but the spirit – that the Sabbath was made for man, not man for the Sabbath. Play on!

## Saints

Think of a saint and we think of haloes and pious poses and exalted achievements, but it is us who have made them into plastercast statues – they were all too human once upon a time, and just as there is always much joy in heaven, so must there also be much laughter in the saint, both living and departed. Laughter and wholeness and holiness all go together.

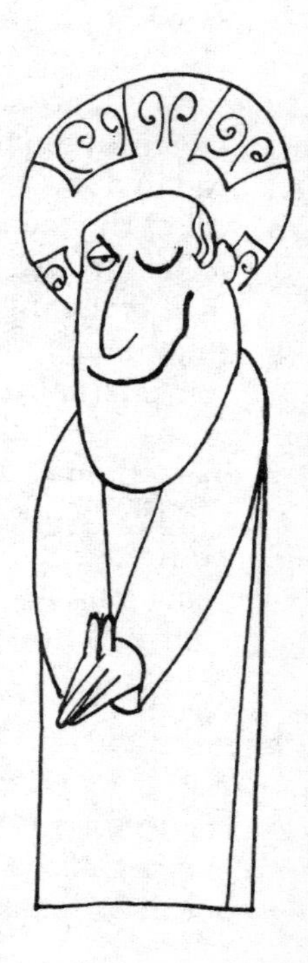

If the clowns had a patron saint, Saint Francis of Assisi would be a leading candidate because it was said of him that laughter followed him wherever he went, while his followers were called his 'joculatores', his merrymakers. Humour and humility are derived from the same word 'humus', meaning the ground or the earth, and saints need to be grounded in order to aspire to the heights. Yet the humour which grounds them and stops them taking themselves too seriously also provides the way of transcendence to rise above the constraints of this world. Saints never believe their own publicity, yet saints and clowns are obviously human and yet somehow not of this world – it produces the paradox of sainthood and the mystery of clowns.

Have you ever seen a statue or a picture of a saint which has him rolling about on the floor clutching his sides in mirth, or her throwing her head back in uproarious laughter? Perhaps it's time you corrected the balance and produced some!

## Silence!

Often thought to be the preserve of mimes, silence matters to clowns and fools too. By and large, in church we are far too wordy. It's almost as if we were conspiring to shut God out of whatever we're doing. And because congregations are not used to silence, it can be frightening at first. When we clergy say 'in a moment or two of silence' we mean silence measured in a few seconds. I measured one the other day. It lasted all of thirteen seconds!

If you are trying to communicate a message, an idea, a story, give it the dignity of time to sink in, give it a chance to be understood, looked at, explored, tasted. Don't rush madly on mistaking speed for business well done. If what you are saying or doing really matters – and if it doesn't, don't do it – then value it with the time and space it deserves.

Use pauses as marvellous chances for meaning, understanding, listening as a new experience. Christians are paying money to learn how to listen. Give them the chance for free and perhaps we'll all hear the voice of God.

## Slapstick

Slapstick has come to mean clowns making a mess but the term comes from an ancient prop that clowns and fools have used for centuries. Made of two slats of wood that slap together it produces the sound effect of a blow or slap without there having to be one. You can make one yourself with two thin slats of wood by inserting an extra piece between the two at one end, which both makes a handle and allows the two slats to slap against each other.

Slapstick fights don't now use slapsticks but a simple variation on the theme: the slap is made by the person being 'hit' as he claps his hands together at the supposed point of impact. You have to clap where the audience can't see you doing it – on their blind side, but you're helped by the fact that the audience's focus will be on your cheek rather then down by your side where you're clapping. It takes practice and timing to get it right, but it needs to look as realistic as possible. The aggressor needs to stop as close to the cheek as he can, while the victim's head needs to jerk back as if hit, but only as far as the force of the blow dictates. If you want to fake a punch, again the fist stops short of the chin, and this time it's the aggressor who makes the sound effect by thumping his chest with his spare fist. If you want to stamp on her foot, just miss by a fraction and you've got the sound effect from your foot hitting the floor, and it's her hopping around on one foot that provides the focus and the comedy – nobody's going to sit there and work out whether you actually stamped on her foot or not! There is a similar effect to be added to falls, because if you slap the ground as you land it sounds and looks much more impressive and dangerous as well as painful. Exaggeration, as always, is the clown's speciality. The good thing about slapstick fights is that nobody gets hurt and there is a cartoon-like quality to the violence.

Why not do a whole fight to illustrate 'an eye for an eye, a tooth for a tooth' and then bring on the referee to stop the fight who begins to explain about loving your enemies. Make sure the ending packs a punch though – how about the referee spreading out both his arms to take applause and knocking out both the fighters by mistake in the process?! Never labour the point – allow punchlines to work for themselves.

## Smile!

Once you're a clown, the chorus of 'Smile! You're supposed to be a clown!' begins to assail if not haunt you. There is a general perception of a clown that he or she is always smiling, laughing and joking, but that is a very limited vision of the clown. Clowns are sometimes happy, sometimes sad, sometimes angry, and so on. You hardly ever find a whiteface or a tramp smiling at all. Clowns should never be equated solely with smiles. When clowns do smile they must be genuine smiles that derive from and provoke pleasure. The peril of having a huge painted smile as part of a clown's make-up is that it is both restricting in the range of emotion that you can present but it is also a huge artificial grin. Ask a three or four year-old to pose for a camera and you get an enormous fixed smile from ear to ear, but there's no mirth or pleasure in it, no twinkle in the eye. You know when a smile is genuine, so try and keep all yours genuine too.

It's not unlike the 'Smile! God loves you!' stickers, with those ear-to-ear grins that are so obviously empty. Sadly the church is too often like some latter-day Malvolio frantically practising smiles in the corner, having taken himself far too seriously for so long he's forgotten how to do it properly. Send in the clowns and we might get some real smiles in the church – and we can make a ceremonial bonfire of all those stickers!

## Stilts

Stilts are great fun to make and to use. I was due to clown with Sandra Pollerman one weekend in a nearby church on a Sunday. The day before, I made some stilts. I used hardwood, the kind you find as a handrail on staircases. It doesn't splinter, which is important if you're hanging on for dear life.

Cut the two uprights to whatever length is right for you, depending on how tall you are. I cut two short lengths of the same wood for the footrests and bolted them with two coachbolts (better than woodscrews) for each platform to the uprights about thirteen inches off the ground. I then took the stilts and tried them out in our village church.

I'm glad I did. Our church has some shiny floor tiles and in no time at all I was doing some high altitude involuntary splits. Back to the drawing board. Finding some old bicycle inner tube, I cut up some pieces to glue to the bottom of the stilts and tried them again on a slippery floor. They worked perfectly and the next morning I became a high church clown!

If you want strive for the heights, you can drill a number of holes in the uprights and gradually move the platforms further and further up the poles. Remember, though, that as your feet move up the stilts, so will your hands and you may need some longer poles. You'll have an interesting time experimenting, I promise.

If you have never walked on stilts before, get some help, someone to walk alongside and keep you roughly upright until you develop some confidence. And for God's sake don't try and run on stilts. It's also worth looking for details of circus skills workshops in your area. Ring your local adult education office.

## Storytelling – a lost art?

We know most of what we know about Jesus, about the patriarchs and prophets and priests and preachers because others have bothered to tell stories about them, and later these stories came to be written down, edited and organised into books. But who is telling stories now that will be remembered in the future?

It's the job of today's Christians to tell stories, our stories, and the old stories in a way which brings them to life for others. Some listeners may have heard the old stories so often they are anaesthetised to their meaning. 'Oh no, not the Good Samaritan again? Can't we have the sower going forth to sow? You haven't told that one yet this year, vicar!' We read stories in church, we don't tell them. Listen to a storyteller working with children. The story comes alive, demands attention. Close your eyes and you are there, in the sun and the dust, or the snow and the ice. Stories are magical in their power to take us out of ourselves, away from the here and now into the then and there. Stories introduce us to other ideas, new insights.

Each of us has a story to tell, is a story being told, a story of how God grips us, calls us, loves us, sustains us. It's the story of Everyman, Everywoman, clowns with enormous feet hesitantly joining a new dance and getting it all wrong but the mistakes are forgiven. We fall and fall again and rise and rise again.

Find a story, any story, practise telling it to a mirror or a tape recorder. Use your arms, your face, your whole body to tell the story, you're the best visual aid you've got and there's no chance you'll leave it behind. See how a story grows in the telling. Improve it, fashion it, throw away the script and live the story in performance. You could amaze yourself and enthral others. Go on, try it!

## Surprise

Clowns, like jack-in-a-boxes, are forever springing surprises. They revel in the unexpected. They love to have twists in their tales. They want to keep us on the edge of our seat before dumping us on the ground in mirth or lifting us out of our seats in terror or acclaim. Clowns must never be totally predictable – there must be enough energy and joie de vivre to make everything a complete surprise for the clown himself and then it can be a total surprise for everyone else too – even if they've seen it before! There should be a 'Good News!' quality to it, where the excitement in giving the news is matched only by the astonishment and celebration that follows. If a clown does a Bible reading, it's no good presenting it in the normal way that reflects the fact that everyone's heard it before – good news is never tired or old, it's fresh and exciting and surprises us once more. Jesus surprised everyone in his lifetime by the things that he taught and did, and the way that he taught and did them. Clowns are foolish enough to follow that example!

## Symbol not structure

Christianity is a blend of head and heart, and the fault of much modern western theology is that it's located behind and above the mouth, in the brain. We seem to have fallen head over heart in love with concepts and structures and rarefied arguments, all of which have their place somewhere in the scheme of things but which leave very many people in the pew quite cold, and we have enough trouble with the heating as it is.

And all around us are the most marvellously solid symbols of our faith, in nature, in art and music, in furniture, in church decoration. The fish, the cross, the angels, the hammer and nails, the loaves and fishes, bread and wine, the sower and the seed, the weeds, the mustard seed, the sun and the moon and the stars. Where were you, O clown, when the morning stars sang for joy? Thirty pieces of silver, the seamless robe and the gambler's dice, the cup of wine, the sponge on a stick. So much to work with, and we tie ourselves in intellectual knots trying to unravel theological problems that aren't even beginning to matter to fellow pilgrims.

There's a world of meaning in symbols. Understood, mediated, explored with love they can be more than empty arguments, they can illustrate and interpret today's anxieties about meaning, value, life, love, forgiveness, foolishness. They are ours to value and enjoy and share.

Why not organise a workshop based around a single grain of wheat, or a mustard seed . . . wow!

## Tears

Tears are said to be the clown's trademark, and rightly so for the clown has the capacity both to cry with laughter and weep with grief. If the definition of the clown as the vulnerable lover means anything it must mean the vulnerability of tears. Tears are nothing to be embarrassed about or apologised for, they're precious. They

express and articulate all those things that we haven't got the words for, and in the silence and action of our tears we can say all that we want to say and a whole lot more besides. Some clowns have stylised tears as part of their greasepainted face, because tears point not just to the attendant possibilities of tragedy alongside the comedy but also to the necessity and presence of compassion. The clown is a compassionate and thus a tearful creature. Clowns should have the capacity not just to make people laugh but to help them cry as well. The best tears are shared tears – to cry alone is awful. Tears are cathartic – they cleanse and soothe and heal.

But clowns inevitably exaggerate tears too. Circus clowns use a length of hose and a squirter to make tears shoot out of their eyes – well, their eyebrows actually! Using a sponge full of water inside a handkerchief, they weep copiously into the aforesaid hankie and then squeeze out the 'tears' onto the floor. But even such ludicrous tears can be effective if there's a genuine sadness beneath all the nonsense. If there is some truth in what's going on, people can identify with the exaggerated situation, but if it is obviously faked emotion as well as spoof tears, they can't.

Clowns in their tears speak of the God of Tears, who cries with us in our grief and laughs with us in our celebrations – the God we can moan to and share a joke with, the God of the crucifixion and resurrection. Who else but God could turn the disastrous tears of Holy Week into the joyful tears of Easter?

## Timing is everything

Well, almost everything. Most sketches and routines are improved by editing. Be ruthless with what you have written or performed. Don't go to the extreme of cutting out every other word when what you really need to do is to remove the whole paragraph!

Many sketches and monologues simply don't hold up. Remember we are competing with highly professional productions on the screen, in the theatre. Just because we perform in a school, a prison, a church or a hospital doesn't mean we have the right to bore a captive audience. They can leave at any time. You'll still see them sitting there but they will have crept away inside their heads and be doing something quite different. This happens in lectures, sermons, after dinner speeches and over-long or badly paced performances. We should not be found guilty of so doing.

Be brave: get someone whose judgement you trust to listen or watch and give an honest opinion of how it might be made more accessible to the audience. Don't be afraid of such an appraisal, it could be a life-saver.

While on the subject of timing and time, timing matters. Jokes and comedy routines rely on good timing. Watch a professional comedian at work. See how timing works, is made to work, the use of pauses, the variation in pace, the build up of tension and its release. And don't forget what an effect the space's acoustic can have on what you're doing. Some venues have such appalling acoustics, it's not possible to deliver fast lines there. Another argument for casing the joint beforehand.

## Touch

In the midst of a society where so many people are isolated either by choice or by circumstance, the clown is called to touch people both emotionally and physically, for the clown's ministry is a ministry of touch. Clowns love to shake hands with people, and even better to hold hands with them. They love to tickle and tease and prod, to hug and to hold. There is no favouritism, for clowns touch the untouchables and those who have never been touched. Just as for the clown nothing and everything is sacred, so he can venture wherever he dares; so no-one and everyone is special, so he can hold hands with any who will hold hands with him.

Play physical games like 'tag' or 'it', and all their variants. Hug Tag is good for touching because the only way to avoid being caught is to hug somebody else – you can't have threesomes, and you can't stay in the corner hugging, but otherwise it's fair game. You can play the various trust games. A classic one is to put people in groups of eight to ten, form a tight circle, and then one person stands in the middle.

She must close her eyes, stay upright but otherwise just allow herself to fall, trusting that she will be caught, and then she is gently pushed around the circle in all sorts of directions.

The Christian faith is based on the incarnation, on the Word being made flesh, and it is vital that we find ways of making it physical once more rather than making do with lots of words. The ministry of touch needs a sensitivity that utilises all of our senses, and that includes our sense of touch and a sense of humour. Fooling is to do with feeling – both physical and emotional. So don't be afraid both to touch and to be touched.

Having said that, beware of people with arthritic hands. I once met a matron in a maternity unit. She put out her hand to shake mine. I grasped it firmly and shook it. In a moment she had vanished and I wondered what on earth I had done. An hour or two later, she reappeared to apologise for putting herself in real pain by allowing me to shake her hand. I know now just how she feels. With arthritis in my knuckles, I find it almost impossible to resist a handshake, it's such a natural thing to do. And the pain can be excruciating!

## Tragedy and comedy

Tragedy and comedy are strange bedfellows. Closely related and seemingly opposite to one another. Tears of grief and tears of laughter issue through the same tear ducts. 'Sometimes I don't know whether to laugh or cry,' says the fool teetering on the edge of a great disaster, yet able to see the funny side. Death and resurrection are tragedy and comedy writ large for the Christian. And one is not possible without the other. No Easter without Good Friday.

Fools and clowns work with tragedy and comedy, the stuff of everyday life. Working with grief is, in part, about coaxing deep feelings to the surface, be they anger or rage at God or some fond memory of the way he would eat porridge even in a heatwave: 'I don't know why he did, but it still makes me laugh.' Dicing with death, putting off the evil moment by rolling dice with all the compulsion of the born gambler, has its comic side. 'Ah, Death! I thought you'd be thinner!' is a line probably as old as comedy itself.

If we really believe that the worst possible tragedy can be redeemed by love, by laughter, then that's what we have to express in the way we clown, the way we fool. Wallowing in gloom won't do, but neither will shallow, frothy, artificial laughter which takes no account of suffering and pain.

Typically, clowns and fools will know both ends of the piece of string, both sides of the coin, and find ways of holding them together in a tension that creates and does not trivialise or destroy.

## Tramp clown

The tramp clown or hobo clown is a classic type of clown but he didn't appear on the scene till the 1920s and 30s. In America the circus had expanded from the traditional European one ring circus to three rings, so that three acts were presented at once. In the midst of all this, clowns started coming on in large groups so that they would be noticed and it seemed the day of individual clowning in the centre of the arena was endangered if not dead. But then, in the days of the Depression in the USA, along came a new clown, echoing as always the society in which he lived, and this was the hobo clown, the sad clown. Charlie Chaplin is the obvious example in films, but it was the likes of Emmett Kelly and Otto Griebling who established the tramp in circus.

He didn't take centre stage, he just appeared on the edges of things and he related to individuals in his own quiet, sometimes forlorn ways, but there was always a twinkle in his eye, there was always fun to be had, the sadness was never terminal. There are angry tramps too, protesters who protest too much, but the sad hobo has the most to offer for gentle and vulnerable clowning. He is the clown who has nowhere to lay his head, the clown who is forever shaking the dust off his feet from one place and moving on to the next, the restless pilgrim disappearing into one sunset only to appear with each new dawn with new hope in his eyes and hopelessness in his gait, hoping against hope that all will be well.

If you want to be a tramp, see **Facepaints** on how to do the make-up, add a few ragged clothes and a battered hat and you're away.

## Trombone

'Love thy neighbour . . . even if he does play the trombone.' The trombone is a comic instrument. Basically an arrangement of bits of plumbing, it is a marvellous prop for almost any kind of fooling. Try putting it together as if you have never seen it before and the laughs can come thick and fast. Play it, as if you've never played it before, and the groans and insults multiply. The cheapest trombones are those made in China. I bought my first one for £30 and the price included case and mouthpiece. The trombone is a great instrument for punctuating, or musically commenting on, the pompous pronouncements of a whiteface or other authority figure. It can produce joyous blasts, sad sliding notes, or one day, please God, in my case, beautiful music. I'm working on it.

A word of warning: children are fascinated by trombones and often want to try to play them. The instrument is easily damaged, so keep a wary eye on adventurous would-be trombonists.

**Danger Box**

The trombone slide, badly managed, can cause serious injury. Not for nothing is the instrument known by bandsmen as the kid-shifter!

In passing it's worth noting that the famous French clown painter Gabriel Loire almost always portrays clowns as carrying a trumpet or bugle. A simple fanfare on a bugle can really spice up an arrival or clown entrance. But whatever you do, don't blow your own trumpet!

## Truthfulness

At the very heart of the clown is a truthfulness that bestows authenticity and authority on him and allows him to speak the truth. The jester was the licensed truth-teller, and the clown in whatever guise has that licence still as long as he remains basically truthful. If you get it wrong, you get your head chopped off, but when you get it right the truth is undeniably proclaimed.

That's why the clown is such an obvious character to speak of the truth, of the good news of God. Amidst all the laughter and tears and lunacy, the truth can still be told and perceived. Your clown character, face and costume must be true to what you are, the stories you tell be true to your story, the words that you speak be true to whatever the situation and whoever the person.

A clown could have fun with a truth detector – it could be like a metal detector, and you eventually alight on the Bible and all the buzzers go off and the lights flash. Or there might be a text in large letters on the wall – the truth detector might explode with excitement, or you could set up an eye test with one eye covered to see if a member of the audience can read it. If the person is game, extend the costume, so that it's a pirate's eye patch and she'll need a parrot on her shoulder, though the parrot isn't allowed to cheat. Try periscopes and telescopes and magnifying glasses, all hidden on your person, and add different bits of silly costumes that each have some meaning, rather like the 'armour of God'. But in the end it's not the reading of it that matters it's what you do about it, whether you clothe yourself in the garments of truth.

What if every person in the land had to put on a jester's cap and bells before reading the Bible in church on a Sunday? Now wouldn't that be something!

## Under-rehearsed, underpaid . . .

If it's under-rehearsed, don't do it. Counsel of perfection? Yes, and why not? Quite apart from any consideration of doing the very best we can, there's the question of safety, of the scandal of being mediocre for Christ's sake!

A factor in under-rehearsal is the crime of being over-ambitious. If you are determined to perform the entire chariot race from Ben Hur, the chances of adequately rehearsing it, given the engagement diaries of horses and charioteers are remote indeed. Better to settle for a total and intentional send-up with the music playing at the wrong speed and assorted clowns driving unseen chariots pulled by equally invisible nags.

And to replay the feeding of the five thousand, strip it to its bare essentials, a pile of paper plates and crowd noises off. You have to believe that people have brought their imaginations with them. If they haven't, you're doomed whatever you do.

If someone can't remember lines, write them out of the script and give them something else to do. If they can't make rehearsals for your wildly funny skit on how St Paul came to write the passage about Jew or Greek, slave or freeman, male or female in Galatians 3, then work with someone who can. For my money, Paul was being massaged by a muscular bondswoman while a Greek scribe penned his words, and each of them wanted to add further categories to the list and were in a strong position to affect the final version!

## Unicycle

The unicycle, the one-wheeled cycle, is a wonderfully improbable means of transport and thus quite fitting to the clown. It's great for entrances and exits and for careering around on, especially up aisles and around cloisters! Once you can do it, then you can start to play on it and make it look even more impossible than it is – that is true of all skills, in that you've got to able to do it well before you can successfully, and thus comically, make them look difficult.

Really the only way to learn the unicycle is to climb on one and keep falling off it. It is just like learning to ride a bike – no-one can do it for you. The only consolation is that once you can travel the first five feet, you can probably do fifty. Here are a few tips. Make sure the seat is the right height – when the pedal is at its lowest, your leg should be slightly crooked. When you get on, make sure there's something or someone to hang on to, put your weight on to the lower pedal, and then swing up to sit on the seat and put your foot on the other pedal. Get the feel of what it is like to be on it by rocking forward and backwards a bit, and maybe if there's someone there, get them to walk you forwards. You've got to sit as erect as you can and treat the unicycle as your bottom half – you don't let your legs run away from you nor do you leave them behind, you travel with them by keeping above them!

Focus on where you want to get to – perhaps the tree twenty yards away. And then you just have to let go, both because it's the only way you're going to learn and to get to the other end, but also because you're going to need both your arms to help you balance. To begin with you'll fall off immediately – there is no avoiding it! Each time you fall, try and grab the front of the unicycle seat as you go, both because it protects your unicycle but also because it helps you get a sense of control as well as keeping you up for longer. To keep moving you have to keep pedalling – as soon as you stop, it will fall. If you lean forward a bit it will move more slowly; if you lean back, it moves more quickly. It is much better to try and lean forward a bit, because we naturally tend to lean back and lose control. By leaning forward a bit you get that forward momentum that you need to both get going and keep going. If you have a good sense of balance, you should be able to make fairly rapid progress but then it takes a lot of practice to get total control. Turning corners is done either by leaning into the turn or by staying upright and using the physical force of a swivel of your hips to turn the wheel beneath you.

To stay on the spot you have to rock forwards and backwards, and once you can do that you can begin to combine skills and do all sorts of things. It is worth the effort but it can be a fairly painful process.

## Ventriloquism

Ventriloquism is an art that seems to have become unfashionable. In a world full of high-tech toys and computer games, the notion of a talking puppet must seem a little quaint! But the art of the ventriloquist is to persuade us that the puppet, be it animal, vegetable or mineral, is alive and talking. Anyone can have a go at it – it's largely a matter of practising how to do the voice and then believing that the voice actually comes from your partner!

Don't rush out and buy an expensive doll or puppet, make one that appeals to you. An ordinary glove puppet can work perfectly well, as long as you have some control over its mouth. If the mouth moves when it's speaking, it helps to foster the illusion that it is the puppet that's speaking.

Obviously you don't want your lips to be moving at the same time, and that's the bit that needs practising, but you can get round that by having your puppet continually whisper in your ear and you relay what the puppet has said to you.

When you try to talk without moving your lips, don't clamp your lips and teeth shut. Allow them to stay open about a quarter of an inch – if it helps, hold a matchstick or cocktail stick between your teeth as you're doing it. The hardest letters to do are B, F, M, P and V, and you just have to fake them by substituting a different but similar-sounding letter. So B becomes D or G, F becomes TH, M becomes N or Ng, P becomes T or K, and V becomes Th. If you don't dwell on the cheated letter, you'll get away with it. If it still sounds terrible to you, substitute a different word that hasn't got the impossible letters in! Or tease the puppet because he can't say it properly or, even better, let the puppet tease you!

Try to keep the puppet moving, even if only slightly. If the puppet stays rigid unless it's actually talking it is lifeless for much of the time – rigor mortis is deemed to have set in! And when it's not talking, keep its mouth closed rather than leave it gaping and gormless. When you're moving the mouth for speech, try and make the lower half of the mouth do the moving. It's natural to want to move the upper half when you open and close your hand, but it's the lower jaw that does the work in speech. And give the puppet a different voice from yours, a voice that fits the character – it might be different in pace or pitch or tone or accent.

The more you look at the puppet the more you direct the audience's attention away from you and towards the puppet. Look as though you're listening to it, be animated and react appropriately. They'll stop worrying about whether you're moving your lips and enjoy watching the puppet instead.

Ventriloquism gives the chance to tell stories from a different angle. It gives people who work solo an opportunity to work with a partner and bounce off them – an apparent source of ideas, brainwaves, and foolish suggestions. If you're an auguste, a whiteface puppet offers all sorts of avenues and possibilities. Why not interview a biblical character who can offer his own point of view? Zaccheus, being small in stature, would be an ideal candidate for a tramp clown puppet . . .

When you're working with puppets, the puppet can move the story on or change the subject completely. It appears that you have no control over them, which again helps the illusion that you're trying to maintain, though sometimes they literally do have a life of their own and you have to go with their inspiration. You are deemed to be mad if you talk to yourself, so perhaps ventriloquism is simply a formalised madness in performance that is ideally suited to the clown. Have a go!

## Vestments

Vestments are basically what some clergy wear when they are performing or presiding or preaching in church. Why not make some with clown motifs on. A chasuble with clowns on doesn't have to be carefully embroidered – it can be made of paper and disposed of, or linen or felt. Make stoles (the scarves that hang around the neck) with a sad clown face on one end and a happy one on the other. Make matching altar frontals and drapes for the lectern and pulpit. How about a paper chain of clowns around the bottom of the surplice –

who needs lace?! I'd love a cope covered in clowns with an empty cross as the central focus, but I don't suppose I'd ever have occasion to wear it!

## Vulnerability

Look at any picture of Jesus on the cross and you see a man at his most vulnerable. He can't fight back, his hands are tied. He can't kick against his tormentors, his feet are nailed. He can curse – whoever had better reason? What does he do? He forgives his executioners, he fixes to meet his fellow victims in paradise and hands his mother over to the care of a friend.

Jesus, man for others, truth telling fool, vulnerable lover, suspended between heaven and earth, God's clown. Offensive? Perhaps. Revealing? Certainly. Whatever else clowns and fools may be, we are vulnerable. What they do to our antics, our jokes, our stories, they do to us and we have to stand there and take it, our only defence being love. Slapped in the face, we turn the other cheek. Knocked down by life's disasters, we always get up knowing that what has happened before will happen again. But we got up before and we'll do that again, knowing that it's possible. Tempted to leave it all, we remain loyal fools.

Most clowns have been poor in the world's eyes. Few fools make their fortunes. But when people laugh at us, laugh with us, laugh at themselves, we know we are blessed with one of God's great gifts, the gift of laughter. Poor, yet making many rich. Vulnerable and yet able to walk the road with others who are vulnerable too, the dying, the sick, the lonely, the unloved, the misunderstood. Truth tellers, we may be mocked and derided.

And when we embrace and carry that vulnerability within ourselves, we live a question mark against the high, the mighty, the proud, the pompous, the self-important, the self-righteous.

If ever there was a clown or foolish pop group . . . how about the MagnifiCats for a name?

## Walks

Finding the way a character walks is vital to the discovery of that character, and it is no less so for clowns. The way you walk is distinctive – it says something about you and the kind of person you are. It's a moving body language that allows us to articulate all kinds of attitudes and emotions without having to voice them. We've tried a way of walking with hats on *(see* **Hats***)* but here are some more.

Warm up by walking normally, but then change into walking in imaginary situations, e.g. in haste, on tiptoe, on the beach, in a hayfield, in the sea. Become different people, such as a head waiter, policeman, pensioner, tramp, accountant, bishop, fashion model, lollipop lady.

Try different physical ways of walking, with feet turned in as far as you can, and then splayed out. Allow the rest of your body to follow suit, especially your arms. Try using physical leads, so that if your forehead is leading you, as if you're being pulled along by a string on your forehead, discover what kind of character that makes you into. Try it at different speeds, turn corners, and establish the appropriate rhythm of the walk. It's a very blinkered way of walking, with no thought apparent. Hence it can be a mindless subservience, or a mindless aggression, or a mindless kind of stupidity. Try being led by your nose (inquisitive), chin (arrogant), chest (puffed up authority), stomach (gross/pregnant), hips (laid back/sexy), knees (ancient/childish). The brackets suggest basic characteristics but there are all sorts of variations. Some physical leads will do something for you, others may not.

Split the group into pairs, and one of the pair sits out to watch how their partner walks. The person should walk as normally as they can, while the partner observes the feel of the walk, the impression and quality of it, as well as the detail, such as how they hold their head or hands, whether one side is different from the other, and so on. Then when they think they've got it, the partner steps in behind and tries to create the walk exactly. Once they've got it, the people behind carry on walking their partner's walk while those in front step aside and see for themselves how they walk – most people are surprised at what they see! Then get back in harness again, only this time the person behind chooses an obvious element of the walk and exaggerates it – the walk still has to work and have rhythm. Then exaggerate a second element of the walk and add that, before finally allowing the person in front to step aside and see what's become of their walk. If the exaggerations are big, bold and playful, they're fun and both the perpetrator and the victim enjoy it. The ones that work best are when the exaggeration is truthful to what is there – it's the clown's art of exaggeration in search of truth again. Once you've finished, swap round and let the victims have their revenge! Lots of clowns in Europe make a living out of slotting in behind people in the street and imitating them – done playfully with sufficient style and exaggeration, it's funny and it speaks quite powerfully. Think what you could do with a clergy procession!

Once you've established the possibility of silly walks, get everyone to create one, making sure they use arms and posture and everything. Then line up the pairs facing each other at opposite ends of a large room. To warm up, get everyone to change ends, using their silly walks. Then on the next trip, just as they pass their partner, they must click into their partner's walk. After a dry run with everyone doing it together, try each pair separately. The change should be instant, and the ones that work best are not only when the walks of the pair are wildly different, but also when the silly walk has obvious character and somehow truthfulness because it makes it much easier to slip into.

## Water

Water in the hands of a clown appears to be a dangerous thing, but it should only ever appear to be so. To soak someone else is never funny, unless it's a fellow performer who is expecting it, and even then it may not be. Clowns can threaten with water – it's part of the clown's armoury. But the delivery should end up as a bucket of confetti or similar, which you have swapped with the real stuff in an identical bucket when no-one was looking. A bit of spray or a small splash never hurt anyone but never go any further than that. If it looks like an accident you're more likely to get away with it, but some clowns have sufficient character and cheek to get away with it on purpose – as long as there is a come-uppance for them too.

You can get yourself wet as much as you like. Water can land on your head, go down your trousers, you can step in a bucket, and so on. Slapstick fights with lots of water or its equivalent are good but only if they're well choreographed and have a logical sequence – again gratuitous water just isn't funny. If you're going to spill a lot of water, make sure that the floor is protected. And make sure you've a change of costume and a towel, if you need them!

## Welcome

First impressions count. Imagine entering a church for the very first time. The people are strange, the interior is unfamiliar. You're handed books you've never seen before and left entirely alone to find a place to sit. All around there's noise and chatter but nobody says a word to you. Suddenly, everyone around you shuffles to their feet and a flock of white robed people, some with funny hats, process into the church. A hymn is announced and people start singing. It's all very strange, unnerving. Should you leave now or stay a

little longer?

Some churches go out of their way to make the stranger and the first time visitor welcome. Others studiously ignore newcomers, leaving them to sink or swim. It's a wonder anyone goes to such churches more than once. Clowns and fools can help visitors feel less strange for no-one can be as strange as the clown or the fool.

If the kingdom of heaven is for all, then surely the local church can try to be a picture of the kingdom, welcoming everyone, making each and every one feel at home. Welcome visitors and even familiar faces with a word or three. By all means use a feather duster but don't go over the top and beware of dandruff or asthma sufferers. Introduce yourself, ask who they are, escort them to a seat. Dust it off first, make sure they've got the books they need and if necessary stay with them to help them know what to do next. A great temptation when visiting unfamiliar places is for clowns and fools to stick together, safety in numbers.

Fight that temptation and concentrate on welcoming people. Aftercare is important too. Don't just vanish at the end of a service, stay and talk. Better still, stay and listen. Help clear up for we are their servants.

## Whiteface

The traditional European whiteface clown is now extremely rare in Britain, but there are still a number around in Europe – where there is a traditional clown troupe there is likely to be a whiteface amongst them. Whiteface is the original clown, and he has always rather resented the arrival and then the ascendancy of auguste. Whiteface is so called because of his white face with its delicate features. His costume was always covered in sequins, stylish and elegant. He wore a short conical hat perched rakishly on his head. Long white stockings and fancy shoes contrasted hugely with the enormous boots of auguste. But they were meant to be opposites. Whiteface is the straight man, the one who takes himself terribly seriously, though there's still the clown's twinkle in his eye. He is bossy and arrogant, pompous and clever. He can do anything, or at least he thinks he can, and certainly do it better than you! He plays a brass instrument, but something like a saxophone rather than the big and ridiculous brass. Whiteface treats auguste like his servant, but he always gets his come-uppance in the end for those who take themselves too seriously can't be taken seriously at all, but it's only those who take themselves too seriously that don't realise it. Classic biblical whitefaces are the scribes and pharisees – those whitewashed tombs of Matthew chapter 23 – and there's plenty of mileage in the juxtaposition of what the pharisees and Jesus had to offer.

American whiteface is rather different from the European model because it's become a combination of whiteface and auguste, with a white base and large auguste features, and the character is much more what we call auguste although the appearance is usually much prettier. The American whiteface doesn't have the arrogance and the bossiness, and is much more playful.

A modern whiteface might not want to sew on a thousand sequins but a stylish costume is all that is required. Even a top hat and tails is a bit dated, but it's that kind of effect that's needed. Augustes need whitefaces, and vice versa – they're natural partners and bounce off each other beautifully. The whiteface may not get the sympathy or the laughs, but he helps to create and increase them. The Church has got plenty of whitefaces both in its pulpits and its pews – they just a need a few augustes to complement them! Whitefaces need to learn to play on street corners and church rotas rather than pray on them – and augustes can help them to do it.

## Wig

Wigs, like hats, can transform the way you look. A wig can help you to develop a completely different clown character. Clown wigs, unless they are very very good, can sometimes be radically improved by simply pulling or cutting out all the 'hair' and threading in short lengths of different coloured wool. My wife gave an early wig of mine this treatment and it was a huge success. Like me, though, it is beginning to bald somewhat and in the same way that I'm getting used to baldness, I'm beginning to wonder just how important a wig really is for my clown or fool.

Costume, wig and make-up are important as means for developing and sustaining your clown character. Clowning and fooling depend on much more than these accessories, important as they are. They depend on imagination, on sensitivity to the audience, on confidence in what you're doing. I'm looking very carefully at how what we learn in costume can be applied the rest of the week around in the home and at work, believing as I do that God calls us to be fools for Christ throughout our lives and not just in performance.

## Worship

Worship matters. And the trick is to combine the very best we can offer with a proper reverence for God and the exercise of humour in expressing what we believe as clowns and fools. Worship demands wide thinking, brainstorming of a high order. For too long worship has been for some a cramping straitjacket which meets a need for security. For others the very familiarity of worship has become stultifying. The same words are said over and over again, the same readings are heard to the point where all meaning has evaporated. For still others it's the familiarity of the words that gives them

the security to adventure and take risks with exploration and meaning.

Worship expresses such a range of emotions: anxiety, rage, love, puzzlement, longing, delight and meets so many needs that clowns and fools need to tread very warily into unfamiliar settings. Sensitivity to others, to local traditions, customs we find strange or unsettling should inform what we do. We are guests as well as servants. We are being trusted with something infinitely precious, people's perceptions of God.

Where possible, make time to discuss with potential hosts what their worship needs are and how we might assist, building on what is already strong and deep. And for everyone's sakes, try to evaluate after the event what hindered and what helped.

Exploring and helping to enliven worship may be one of the most urgent tasks facing the church and we are privileged when asked to contribute something from the clown and fool perspective.

## Yes

'Yes' is what the true clown always says. He'll try anything, the eternal volunteer, the only one who steps forward when nobody else will dare. He needs to take risks for it is the stuff of life, and what he finds just over the precipice is another one, and then another one, and another one. The true clown says, 'Here am I. Send me', while the rest of us are content to shout, 'Here am I. Send her!' For the clown nothing is impossible – the response is always 'Yes. Of course'.

If you're out clowning and someone suggests something, agree with them, see where it leads, try it. There's a good working motto of 'Use what you're given' – those are the godsends. The ability to say 'yes' allows spontaneity and forces us to dig into our foolish selves and resources and allow all sorts of wonderful things out and surprising things to happen.

'Yes. Let's' is a fun game, and good practice! Everyone gets in a circle. Somebody starts with the suggestion: 'Hey everybody, let's be elephants', for instance, and everybody shouts back as enthusiastically as possible, 'Yes. Let's', and immediately they become elephants! It moves on to the next person in the circle, who might decide 'Hey everybody, let's be sausages!', and so 'Yes. Let's', and everyone becomes sausages. It can get quite surreal! It's worth having someone in charge who can give the nod to the next person at the appropriate point. If it's done fairly quickly it builds up a hilarious momentum. If it's moans, shrieks, groans and laughter you want, try it. It breaks down a few barriers and helps shed a few inhibitions too – it's hard to stand on ceremony or dignity when you've just been rolling around the floor being a sausage! Why not try it? 'Yes. Let's!'

## Zoo games

Zoo games are great levellers. Encourage participants to think of an animal, any animal from an aardvark to a zebra and then become that animal. Go for the full works, a range of expressions from delight and pleasure through boredom to anger. Tell people they can go the whole hog, all the animal noises and actions, scratching, stretching, sniffing, preening, grooming, picking insects off each other.

Then suggest that if they've been a really large animal, an elephant, say, turn into an ant or a woodlouse. If they've been an ant, try a giraffe or a hippopotamus for size. It's a matter of stretching imaginations, leaving their workaday selves behind and trying something totally different and perhaps quite strange. It's about play and playfulness.

Change the situations from the safety of a jungle full of animals to a typical office party full of animals. This may be more familiar ground to some! Or have all your animals go in a party to a Shakespeare play, or a formal dinner, maybe a church service! Encourage them to react to one another. Then either relax and get them to play back how they felt. Was it scary? Did they enjoy becoming the animal or insect? Did they feel real fear or real enjoyment at escaping briefly from their humanity?

Zoo games can be a step on the way towards exploring the child inside or a clown character for the first time. Once you've become an ant-eater, a clown should pose no problems.

zzZZZ

## Bibliography


Roly Bain, *Fools Rush In*, London: Marshall Pickering 1993

Reg Bolton, *Circus in a Suitcase*, Bath: Butterfingers

Reg Bolton, *New Circus*, London: Gulbenkian Foundation 1987

Richard Boston, *An Anatomy of Laughter*, London: Collins 1974

Richard Buckner, *The Joy of Jesus*, Norwich: Canterbury Press 1993

Hovey Burgess, *Circus Techniques*, New York: Brian Dube Inc 1979

Alastair V Campbell, *Rediscovering Pastoral Care*, London: DLT 1981

Norman Cousins, *Anatomy of an Illness*, New York: Norton 1979

Harvey Cox, *The Feast of Fools*, New York: Harper and Row 1970

JG Davies, *New Perspectives on Worship Today*, London: SCM 1978

Umberto Eco, *The Name of the Rose*, London: Picador 1984

Bruce Fife, *Creative Clowning*, Colorado Springs: Java 1988

Dave Finnigan, *The Complete Juggler*, Bath: Butterfingers 1992

Patrick Forbes, *The Gospel of Folly*, Angel Press 1988 (available from the author at 14 East Street, Lilley, Luton, Beds, LU2 8LP)

Michael Frost, *Jesus, the Fool*, Albatross Books (Australia) 1994, available from Lion Publishing

Edward Hays, *Holy Fools and Mad Hatters*, Kansas: Forest of Peace 1993

Robert Holden, *Laughter the Best Medicine*, London: Harper Collins 1993

Arthur Koestler, *The Act of Creation*, London: Picador 1975

Mark Liebenow, *Is there Fun after Paul?*, California: Resource Publ. 1987

Janet Litherland, *The Clown Ministry Handbook*, Colorado: Meriwether 1982

Janet Litherland, *Everything New and Who's Who in Clown Ministry*, Colorado: Meriwether 1993
Wes McVicar, *Clown Act Omnibus*, Colorado: Meriwether 1987
Raymond Moody, *Laugh after Laugh: the Healing Power of Humour*
Colin Morris, *The Hammer of the Lord*, London: Epworth Press 1973
Henri JM Nouwen, *Clowning in Rome*, New York: Doubleday 1979
Stephen Pattison, *A Critique of Pastoral Care*, London: SCM 1988
Perrone & Spata, *Send in His Clowns*, Colorado: Meriwether 1985
Cal Samra, *The Joyful Christ*, New York: Harper Collins 1986
John Saward, *Perfect Fools*, Oxford: OUP 1980
Floyd Shaffer, *If I were a Clown*, Minneapolis: Augsburg 1985
Shaffer and Sewall, *Clown Ministry*, Colorado: Group Books 1984
Richard Snowberg, *The Caring Clowns*, La Crosse, Wisconsin: Visual Magic 1992
Mark Stolzenberg, *Clown for Circus and Stage*, New York: Sterling 1983
Susan Kelly Toomey, *Mime Ministry*, Colorado: Meriwether 1986
John H Towsen, *Clowns*, New York: Hawthorn 1976
Elton Trueblood, *The Humour of Christ*, London: Libra 1964
Enid Welsford, *The Fool, His Social and Literary History*, New York: Doubleday 1961
Jack Wiley, *Basic Circus Skills*, California: Solipaz 1984
William Willeford, *The Fool and his Sceptre*, London: Edward Arnold 1969
Harry Williams, *Tensions*, Glasgow: Fount 1989
Prue Wilson, *My Father took me to the Circus*, London: DLT 1984
Patty Wooten, *Hearts, Humour and Healing*, California: Commune-a-Key 1994

HUMOUR
THEOLOGY
St MATTHEW
St MARK
St LUKE
St JOHN

## Useful addresses

### Roly Bain
285 North Street
Bristol
BS3 1JP

### Patrick Forbes
14 East Street
Lilley
Luton
Beds
LU2 8LP

### Holy Fools
John Saunders
(Membership Secretary)
22 Shalstone Road
London
SW14 7HR

### World Clowns Association
Derek Brazil (Secretary)
10 Burnett Road
Trowbridge
Wiltshire
BA14 0QA

### Clowns International
Blue Brattle (Secretary)
30 Sandpiper Close
Marchwood
Southampton
Hants
SO4 4XN

### The Clowns' Church: Holy Trinity Church, Dalston
c/o The Vicar
Forest House
89 Forest Road
London
E8 3BL

### The Clowns' Gallery
1 Hillman Street
Hackney
London
E8 1DY
(Open first Friday of every month 11am-4pm or by arrangement with Fizzie Lizzie ☎ 0171-723 3877)

## Drama books from National Society/Church House Publishing

### Acting Up £5.95

*Dave Hopwood*

Raps, narrated mimes, response stories, entertaining monologues and more traditional sketches, specially written for performance by or to children in family services, school assemblies or as street theatre.

**Dave Hopwood** is a freelance Christian drama worker and regularly runs training events, conferences, evening courses and workshops all over the country.

### Scenes and Wonders £4.95

*Paul Powell*

Rib-tickling sketches to refresh the parts other drama collections don't reach. Properly cred, they are particularly suitable for teenagers and students.

**Paul Powell** is one of the main scriptwriters for *Spitting Image*.

### Plays on the Word £5.95

*Derek Haylock*

A popular collection of nineteen humorous drama sketches (including eight for Christmas).

*The best sketch is 'A Window in the Diary' where two yuppies discover they have some time available to fit in a Christmas service and phone the vicar to tell him what kind they'd like.*
**YOUTHWORK magazine**

### Sketches from Scripture £4.95

*Derek Haylock*

Fast-moving drama sketches designed to be performed with minimum rehearsal.

# The National Society

*A Christian Voice in Education*

The National Society (Church of England) for Promoting Religious Education is a charity which supports all those involved in Christian Education – teachers and school governors, students and parents, clergy and lay people – with the resources of its RE centres, archives, courses, conferences and publications.

Founded in 1811, the Society was chiefly responsible for setting up the nationwide network of Church schools in England and Wales and still provides grants for building projects and legal and administrative advice for headteachers and governors. It now publishes a wide range of books, pamphlets and audio-visual items, and two magazines, *Crosscurrent* and *Together with Children*.

For further details of the Society or a copy of our current resources catalogue, please contact:

The National Society
Church House
Great Smith Street
London
SW1P 3NZ

Telephone: 0171-222 1672
Fax: 0171-233 2592